Neurons and Narratives

A Teen Brain Operator's Manual

Mark Linsenbardt

First Edition

ISBN: 979-8-9985938-2-6

Published independently by Mark Linsenbardt

Contents

Before You Start

Maybe someone handed you this book. Maybe you heard about it. Or maybe you picked it up yourself because something wasn't working and you couldn't quite explain why. Those are all good reasons to be here. This book is for any of them.

What this book does: It explains what's happening inside your brain during this time in your life, why the strategies that used to work have started costing you things you can't see, and what the path out looks like from here. It's not a lecture and it's not taking anyone's side. You'll meet a kid named Marcus and follow him across about four months of figuring this out. We won't figure it all out at the same time, nobody does, but little by little we will see how it *can* work.

If you picked this up because something feels off and you can't quite name it, that instinct is the right one. The feelings that:

- Things keep going sideways in ways you can't fully account for
- The explanations you have don't quite cover the results you're getting
- Something is running that you're not fully in charge of

Those feelings are what this book is about. They have names and explanations and, more importantly, there is something you can do about them.

One thing to know going in: this book is honest about what's hard.

It's not going to promise that if you do the work everything gets easy, because that would be dishonest and you'd see through it anyway. What it is going to show you is that:

- The situation is more workable than it probably feels right now

- The things running in the background aren't permanent

- The window you're in right now is the specific one designed for exactly this kind of rebuild

That's enough setup. The book starts on the next page.

CHAPTER ONE

Your Brain Was Built for Stories

The lawyer, the autopilot, and the program you didn't write

Marcus had proof.

His stepdad was a jerk, his teacher had it out for him, his mom always took everyone else's side. His biological father kept canceling plans, which honestly wasn't even worth arguing about anymore.

At fourteen, Marcus had a complete and total explanation for why his life was the way it was, and that explanation never once included Marcus. His brain had already built the whole case before anyone asked. Every piece of evidence was filed, every argument from the other side was full of bull, and adults who tried to push back would just talk and talk without ever actually saying anything. Every time something went wrong the story got updated, and Marcus moved on without any idea there was a problem.

Take the Friday his English teacher handed back essays. Marcus got a C. He looked it over, saw the comments, and his brain processed the whole thing in about one second. Ms. Patterson never liked the way he wrote, his words were always the wrong ones, and whatever he turned in was never going to be good enough for her. The grade wasn't about the essay, it was about *her*.

Marcus turned the paper over face-down and moved on. This case was closed. The story got updated, and Marcus went on about his day without any idea there was a problem. He wasn't wrong that Ms. Patterson had preferences, teachers do, and grading does have a gray area, and everyone knows it. His brain found two real pieces of evidence, built a pretty solid case on them, but skipped right over the third piece: Marcus had in fact written the essay the night before it was due and hadn't read a single word afterwards.

The story in his head about Ms. Patterson not liking him did all the work. For Marcus, all of this was just plain and simple truth.

* * *

The First Superpower

Go back far enough in human history, past your great-grandparents, past the first schools and cities, past written language entirely, and you find yourself in a world where your ancestors lived in small groups around campfires and in caves. They didn't have books, or phones, they didn't even have words written down anywhere. But they had stories, oh yes, they had stories.

Picture this: it's maybe twelve thousand years ago and it's lightly snowing. One of your ancestors is walking across an open field and spots tracks in the snow or the mud, this time they are deer tracks, and they are fresh ones! His brain does something remarkable right then. It tells itself a story about the future, almost like a kind of mental time travel.. So this cave dude knows the deer has to get to water, and he knows there's a cliff that will get there faster, and deer can't climb, but he can. He builds this story in his head in basically three parts:

1. The deer is headed toward water
2. I can climb the cliff and get there first
3. Once I am there, this is what I will do next

Then he acts on a story that hasn't happened yet.

Every other animal on Earth responds to what's right in front of it. Your ancestor responded to a story he built in his own head. He climbed the cliff, waited, and ate that night because his brain could build a narrative and run it forward in time.

Plus, cave dudes lived in groups, so when this fancy pants (without pants) hunter brings the deer back to the cave a DIFFERENT story is told. The hunter tells everyone about how he was just hangin" by the water, when this deer came up and tried to stick him with the antlers, so then they brawl, and he tells everyone how he kicks the deer's ass, and kills it, and then, because he is super cool, he brings the meat back for everyone in the cave.

So first, we learned to tell stories to ourselves, act on them, and try to create results from them. Then we learned to tell stories to others and try to create results from those.

That's how humans got to the top of the food chain.

The storyteller was the most important person in every tribe across every culture that's ever existed. More important than the strongest fighter, or the Chief, or the Queen, or even the Medicine Man. Because the storyteller kept the tribe's history alive, taught children what mattered, and explained why things happened.

Stories were the original history books, and everything the tribe knew got passed down through them. Then we invent this whole idea of writing things down and boom, we get written stories, and those become recorded history.

Generations of stories wired something into the human brain that's still happening in yours right now.

Your brain thinks in stories. Ask someone to tell you about themselves and they tell you a story, ask them what happened yesterday and they tell you a story, beginning, something goes wrong, resolution: three parts, every time, everywhere on Earth, in every culture that's ever existed. The basic structure is the same because the wiring is the same.

Here's the part that matters for you right now: when something happens to you, good, bad, confusing, unfair, your brain's first move is to build a story about it.

Not gather evidence, not stay neutral, not wait for more information. Build a story and build it *fast*.

That story has three important characters that are there every time. They are present in every movie you've ever watched, every TV show, lots of songs, even school plays. They are the Good Guy, the Bad Guy, and the Victim. (Good Girl, Bad Girl, Victim are exactly the same, internal stories adapt to our own gender without any thought) Your brain casts those roles automatically, and it has a very strong preference for where it puts you, which is to say you have a favorite role.

* * *

The Lawyer in Your Head

Think about a lawyer whose only job is to make sure you look okay. Every hour of every day, all they do is protect the client, which is YOU.

This lawyer doesn't care about truth or fairness or whether you were actually right or wrong. Nope, that is not what a lawyer does. The *only* job is: protect the client.

When something good happens, the lawyer is there right away, documenting evidence of how cool you are, and preparing the best ways to tell the story so that you will get the best results from various people depending on how you tell the story.

When something bad happens, this lawyer jumps into action immediately. Evidence that helps you gets highlighted, evidence that hurts you gets buried. Your role in the situation gets smaller, the other person's role gets bigger. Timing gets adjusted a little, tone gets reread a different way, and the story that comes out puts you in the best position available. Then the lawyer hands it to you as: "here's what really happened."

You believe it, of course you believe it, it was your brain that built it.

This isn't stupidity or pride either, it's efficiency. Your brain evolved to protect your life and your position in the group. For most of human history, being seen as the problem, the liability, or the one who couldn't be trusted, was genuinely dangerous. People who got pushed out of the group didn't survive. So the brain developed a standing defense: *never* **be the villain in your own story.**

Don't for a second think that adults don't do this, because we do. Your parents are running the exact same program. They have their own lawyer in their head building their own case, and their lawyer is just as good at its job as yours. When you and a parent are in an argument, there are two lawyers in that room, and both of them are absolutely convinced their client is right.

Look, that's not some kind of flaw in anyone's character, that is just how brains work. One difference is that your parent is also in the role of judge. That's how they see it, because they spent years judging what the best things for you are and those programs are well established. The funny thing is… you used to see it that way too.

Here's what that looks like in a real situation. Your stepdad says you left dishes in the sink again. Your brain doesn't pause, it immediately gets to work. It notes that your stepsister also left dishes yesterday and nobody said anything, it notes that his tone was a little harsh just for dishes, and it notes that this always happens when he's had a rough day. Your lawyer builds a case: "This isn't really about dishes, this is about him taking out a bad day on you, again."

That whole case gets built in about one second. It might even have some true parts in it. It definitely leaves some stuff out, like the dishes *were* yours, and you *did* leave them there.

The lawyer built you an exit from that before you even knew you needed one. Now you're in an argument about his tone and the double standard and whether this is fair, and somewhere underneath all of it, the dishes are still in the sink.

The question now is if you recognize it happening, or let it keep running in the background without ever stopping to look.

* * *

How the Case Gets Built

The lawyer doesn't start from scratch every time something goes wrong. It draws from a file it's been building your whole life.

Think about a story you've told yourself enough times that it stopped feeling like a story. Maybe it's something about how teachers always single you out, or how your family never really listens, or how you never catch a break, or how you're just not a school person.

That story didn't arrive fully formed, it got built piece by piece from experiences that the lawyer filed under: [EVIDENCE] Proof of Your Truth.

One teacher was unfair. Filed: teachers are unfair. Second teacher was unfair. Filed: the brain lawyer decides this is a pattern, "teachers are unfair". Then the third teacher is actually fair, but maybe a little too demanding. It gets filed anyway under the same category because that's how it works. Your brain doesn't search for truth, it searches for proof that the story it already has is correct.

Once a story has enough evidence behind it, it stops feeling like an opinion and starts feeling like fact. At that point it doesn't even need to think anymore. A situation happens, the conclusion arrives before you've processed anything, and the story writes itself.

That's where Marcus was. His stories were old enough and well-sourced enough that they ran without effort. His stepdad did something and his brain filed it under: stepdad is a jerk. His teacher would say something and his brain would file it under: she has it out for me. The whole system was so automatic that Marcus didn't experience it as storytelling at all. He experienced it as seeing things clearly, which of course is why nobody else gets it, and nobody else *gets him*.

Everyone who runs this long enough eventually ends up in that same place. The story becomes invisible because like looking through a telescope, the story becomes the lens. You're not telling yourself a story anymore, you're just seeing reality. Except you're not.

* * *

Why We Call It Drama

The stories your brain builds aren't random. They follow that same three-part structure with the same three required characters: Good Guy, Bad Guy, Victim.

Your brain doesn't just use this structure for movies, it uses it to cast everyone in your actual life. When something goes wrong between you and another person, your brain assigns those three roles in about half a second, and it has a very strong preference: it puts you in the Good Guy or Victim position and hands the Bad Guy role to whoever is most available.

The Victim role sounds bad, but it really delivers something useful, it takes away all responsibility. If you're the victim, nothing is your fault, you didn't cause this, you're just the one it's happening to.

The Good Guy role sounds better, but it comes with the same exit from accountability built in. If you're the reasonable one, the one who's trying, the one who's justified, there's nothing for you to look at or change. You're already doing it right.

The Bad Guy role, the one your brain always assigns to someone else, does all the work of explaining the situation: the teacher who has it out for you,the stepdad who crossed a line, the friend who went behind your back, the parent who never listens.

Once you have a bad guy, the story has a cause, and that cause is outside of you.

A psychologist named this the Drama Triangle, good guy, bad guy, victim, and the important thing to understand is that it doesn't feel like drama from inside. It feels like clarity, it feels like correctly reading what's really going on. The roles get assigned so fast and feel so right that most people never notice they're in a structure at all.

Watch any argument between two people. Both of them think they're the good guy or the victim. Both of them have handed the bad-guy role to the other person, and BOTH of them have evidence. Both lawyers are doing their jobs. Two completely different stories about the same event, both of them feeling like the accurate one. The *complete* truth might not be in either story.

That's literally why, when we see people doing this, we call it drama. That's where the word comes from. The triangle, the three roles, the automatic casting. It's been running in humans for as long as we've been telling stories around campfires. You didn't invent it and neither did your parents. It's just the operating system.

The Program Running Without You

There's a difference between something you're doing and something that's running automatically.

When you *decide* to do something, consciously, in the moment, that's you. When a program runs based on conditions your brain set up years ago, before you had any say in how it got designed, that's the autopilot, that's a program running.

Think about learning to ride a bike. The first time, you were thinking about every single thing at once. You had to focus on balance, pedaling, steering, and not falling over. Your brain was working hard. Every time you practiced, the pathway for 'riding bike' got a little faster and a little more automatic. Once you gave the process enough repetitions, this stuff called myelin coated the pathways in your brain. Myelin is a substance that works like insulation on a wire, it makes the signal travel faster and cleaner. Now, you get on a bike and just ride, you don't think about it. The program just runs.

Your responses to hard situations got built the same way. The first time something difficult happened and you deflected or pulled back or performed, THAT was a choice, maybe an instinctive one, but there was friction. Your brain was working it out. Every time after that, the pathway got faster, more automatic, less like a choice and more like just what you do.

By the time you're fourteen, a lot of those pathways are established and well-coated. They fire before you think, before you have a chance to choose anything else. That's how brains are built, every brain works this way including your parents.

Your brain builds programs the same way it builds stories, out of what happened repeatedly. Every time a behavior produced a useful result the brain noted it. Every time a response worked, reduced tension, avoided pain, got you what you needed, the brain strengthened that pathway. Do it enough times and it becomes automatic.

You didn't write the program, it was written from your experience, back when you were a kid, mostly in situations you didn't choose, around people you never picked. By the time you were old enough to have an opinion about any of it, this programming was already running.

Deflection is a program. So is withdrawal, performing, controlling, and shutting down. These aren't personality traits, they're solutions the brain stuck in a file called **This Worked** The brain doesn't evaluate whether a solution is healthy or fair or likely to work in ten years. It only asks one question: did it work? If the answer is yes, keep it.

Marcus's deflection program started running long before ninth grade. His biological father canceling again and again created an early story: "Pain can come from outside sources, and there's nothing I can do about it."

His stepdad is another example. Dude just showed up and was given authority over him without anybody asking if that was ok, so that made another story: "Authority imposed without consent is wrong."

A few early arguments where deflecting caused someone to back off filed the strongest story of all: "OH! this works for arguments, this is how you win."

By fourteen the program was fast. It didn't feel like a strategy or even a response. It just felt like being Marcus. He was calm like someone who already knows what will happen, whose brain has already processed the situation and reached a verdict before the conversation started. His brain had decided who he was, decided who everyone else was, and was just collecting evidence to confirm it.

Nothing crazy was happening, the program was just running.

* * *

Why They Used to Send Kids Away

For a long time, before anyone understood any of this science, parents and societies noticed that teenagers who got sent away, came back different.

Neurons and Narratives

Military schools. Boarding schools. Trade apprenticeships where a thirteen-year-old got handed off to a blacksmith or a carpenter in another town and lived there, worked there, and learned there. These weren't just about education, they were spurts of growth. People didn't fully understand why they worked, but they worked.

Here's why it worked, in terms your brain can actually use: When you arrive somewhere completely new, all the old programs stop working at the same time. New people who don't know your story and don't owe it anything. New authority figures who didn't watch you grow up and aren't going to make exceptions. New social groups where your old reputation doesn't exist yet. New rules, new goals, and new situations your autopilot has never seen before.

The old programs have nothing to grab onto. Deflection doesn't work the same way with people who don't already believe your version of events. Your usual moves don't produce the usual results, and because the brain only keeps what works, it immediately starts building new ones, because it has no other choice.

That's accidental neuroscience. Nobody designed it that way on purpose, but it worked because it forced the brain to rewire fast. The environment changed everything before the old programs even had time to dig in deeper.

Most people reading this book aren't getting sent to military school, and you certainly aren't going to get apprenticed to a blacksmith. Which means the forced reset isn't coming. The old programs are going to keep running unless something makes them stop, and that something has to be you. That's not fair, we're not going to pretend it is, but it is the situation.

We'll come back to exactly how that works. For now, just understand that it's possible, and that the people around you who seem like they've got it figured out didn't just wake up that way. Their brains somehow got forced into new territory, or they found a way to do it themselves.

* * *

What the Story Costs

A story that protects your feelings today has a cost that comes later.

Example: Two students fail the same test. Student one thinks: "The teacher is unfair." Student two thinks: "I didn't study right."

Student one keeps their pride intact for the moment. Student two doesn't.

Student one also doesn't change anything, because if the teacher is the problem there's nothing for them to do. They study the same way next time, and fail again. The story absorbs the failure, protects them from the uncomfortable part, and they arrive at the next test prepared in the same way as the last one.

Student two has a really bad moment, because owning something feels like standing exposed out in the open. It's uncomfortable. Because it means the problem was theirs, but so is the solution.

They study differently, the next test goes better. Without announcing itself, a track record gets built for student two that student one will never build. The difference isn't intelligence, it's what their own story left them to work with.

Adults around you recognize this even when they don't say it out loud. Teachers stop going to bat for students whose story is always someone else's fault. They've decided there's no way in. Parents start managing rather than trusting. Friends learn to agree with you or say nothing. You end up surrounded by people who either go along with the story or keep their distance.

Here's how it played out for Marcus specifically. His stepdad tried for about a year and a half. He showed up to games, asked questions, made some bad calls, said the wrong thing sometimes, and pushed when he should have backed off. He was putting in some effort, he was trying. But Marcus's lawyer filed every wrong call and built a case: **Stepdad isn't worth engaging with.** So Marcus stopped engaging.

His stepdad didn't stop trying because he's a jerk. He stopped trying because every time he tried to connect it got deflected, and eventually that math becomes clear: "The effort costs something and produces nothing."

A damaging little program written by his own Lawyer…which he bclicvcd, so he started managing Marcus rather than reaching him. More rules, less conversation.

Marcus experienced the change as confirmation. "See, I was right, he doesn't really care, he's just here to be in charge."

The story was sealed. Every response to the strategy got filed as *more* evidence that the strategy was right (and human beings LOVE to be right).

That's the mechanism. The story creates behavior, the behavior produces a response, the response gets filed as evidence, the story strengthens. Life goes on as before. The world just gets a little smaller.

* * *

The Part Nobody Tells You

This chapter isn't here to tell you your feelings are wrong. That would be crazy. When someone is unfair to you, that's real. When something genuinely isn't your fault, that's real too. The lawyer doesn't only get it wrong, it sometimes gets it exactly right.

For example this story about Marcus is just a story, and in another story the stepdad might actually be a jerk!, but even if that is true, it changes nothing for us. – *keep reading*.)

The problem isn't the story. The problem is the story running without you *knowing* it's just a story.

Your brain is right sometimes, the program reads the situation correctly, the story it builds is accurate, and your lawyer is actually presenting the facts. But other times it gets it completely wrong, and here's the part that you really want to pay attention to: *your brain doesn't know the difference.*

It can't tell you which times are which. It just runs a program and hands you a result *labeled* as truth.

It doesn't know the difference, and unless you stop and look carefully, neither will you.

So the unfair part is this: without getting shipped off to a boarding school or handed to a blacksmith in another town, you have to find a way to write new programs into your brain yourself, and then hold them long enough that they not only become automatic, but they also signal to everyone around you that you're a completely different person.

The people around you have their own programs running, and their programs are looking for evidence about who you are. New behavior has to show up consistently enough that their lawyer starts filing it as evidence under: **Something Changed**.

That takes patience, more patience than feels fair. We're going to come back to exactly how it works later in this book. For now, what matters is knowing that it is possible, and that it starts with questions the autopilot never asks:

1. When something goes wrong, what story does your brain hand you?

2. What role do you most often assign yourself?

3.   What did the lawyer leave out?

Those three questions, asked honestly and with some regularity, will tell you more about how your brain is running your life than almost anything else in this book. They interrupt your program long enough for the real you to show up.

Marcus was going to learn this. Things had to get worse first, and we'll get to that,but the questions are yours right now, if you want them.

* * *

Next: How Your Brain Learned What It Learned

CHAPTER TWO

How Your Brain Learned What It Learned

The rule your brain wrote before you could talk, and why it's still calling the shots right now

Picture a baby alone in a crib, in a dark room, with no idea where it is, no words for anything happening in its body, no way to make sense of any of it.

Something gets cold, or the stomach gets empty, or the silence just feels wrong, and something tightens in the chest, and the baby cries, pure body reaction, no plan behind it, just the body doing what it does when it gets overwhelmed.

Then the room changes. Somebody shows up, arms come, warmth comes back, some food maybe, and whatever was wrong stops being wrong. The baby has zero understanding of what just happened, but the brain makes one fast, unannounced, permanent note: "this behavior solved the problem." (Crying got me what I wanted.)

That's the first lesson your brain ever learned, and it has been using that exact same logic every single day since.

* * *

The Only Rule Your Brain Cares About

Your brain, for all its complexity, uses basically one rule when it comes to deciding what to keep and what to throw away.

Did it work?

That's the whole thing, and it sounds simple until you understand what "work" means to your brain, cause it doesn't mean what you might think it means. Your brain never asks if something was a good idea, or fair, or going to build you a better life in five years. It's always only asking one thing: "Did it work? - did the uncomfortable feeling stop?"

If yes, lock it in, keep it, use it again.

That matters a great deal because your brain was built for survival, and in a survival world, discomfort didn't mean you were having a bad day, it meant something was dangerous. Cold meant you might freeze, hunger meant you might starve, being pushed out of your group meant you might not make it on your own. So, your brain developed a system that worked brilliantly for that world: when something makes a bad feeling stop, remember it, because that thing just kept you alive.

Relief became the signal. Relief is what your brain is always chasing, because relief is what survival feels like.

So when the baby cried and the world rearranged itself, that went into the collection. When a toddler threw a fit and got what they wanted, in it goes. When a kid went still during an argument and the adults backed off, that got stored. When a teenager deflected blame onto someone else and the conversation moved on, BOOM, tag that as a winner. Every single time a behavior made a bad feeling stop, your brain made a note: **This works. Keep this.**

It never once stopped to ask if it was building something worth having. That question is one you have to ask. Your brain just keeps the notes.

* * *

How the Wiring Gets Built

In Chapter One we talked about myelin, the substance that coats pathways in your brain and makes signals travel faster, and here's where that really matters, because this is how any rule stops being a choice and becomes a reflex.

The first time you do something, the signal in your brain travels a thin little trail, like walking through tall grass for the first time, you can barely see where you went and by tomorrow it might be totally gone. Do it again, and the trail gets a little more visible. Do it enough times and your brain decides this path is worth investing in, so it wraps that pathway in myelin, which works like insulation on a wire and makes the signal travel faster and cleaner, and at some point the behavior stops feeling like something you choose and really becomes something that just happens.

Repetition, myelin, automatic. You used a response enough times that your brain paved a road for it, and now that road is always going to be the easiest one to take.

Think about learning a new language. You can take the class, study the grammar, memorize vocabulary, understand the rules perfectly, and still be completely lost when you have to use it. But take someone who really wants to learn and drop them somewhere nobody speaks their language and nobody can interpret, and they learn faster than they ever thought they could, because the environment stopped buffering the gap between what they know and what they need. The brain builds the wiring when it has no other option.

Same thing happens with a new job. Two people start in the same position. One gets a trainer who walks them through everything step by step, covers for their mistakes, answers every question before it becomes a problem.

The other one starts at a small operation that's understaffed and moving fast, gets handed the basics, and is expected to perform. That second person really wanted this job, maybe worked hard to get it, and now they're on their own. What do they do? They ask questions the first person never asks, because the first person has someone to absorb the not-knowing. They look things up outside of work hours. They practice tasks on their own, creating repetition their trainer isn't generating for them. They build the wiring faster, because the environment required them to direct their own learning, rather than waiting for someone to deliver it. The brain builds roads from use, and that second person is using the roads constantly because the stakes are real and they want what's on the other side.

But listen, your brain paves those roads for bad habits just as fast as good ones, faster sometimes, because bad habits tend to produce relief faster, and relief, as we just covered, is exactly what your brain is always chasing.

Avoidance builds myelin just as fast as effort does, blame gets paved right alongside honesty, deflecting,shutting down, and disappearing all get the same investment as showing up and telling the truth, sometimes more, because the relief that comes from avoiding something hard is immediate and obvious, and your brain absolutely loves immediate and obvious. It's completely neutral about where these roads lead, it just paves the ones that you use the most.

* * *

Rules You Never Got to Vote On

The first programs your brain wrote, the first lessons it locked in, the first roads it started paving, all of that happened before you had any say in the matter, and those rules got written by the situation you were born into, the people who were around you, and whatever happened to work in that specific environment. You were basically a learning machine running experiments around the clock, and your brain was storing results with complete indifference to whether those results were going to serve you ten years down the road.

A kid who grew up with a lot of chaos might learn that staying small and invisible reduces danger, so that gets locked in. A kid who got attention when they had big emotions learned that feeling things loudly moved people, and that went into the collection. A kid who saw the adults around them model deflection learned that deflection was the right response to being wrong about something, and that got stored away too. *(That's a really good one, because it demonstrates a program that got filed, and that kid never even tried it, they just saw a parent demonstrate the pattern, and they recorded it for use later)*

Every kid's first classroom was the environment they were born into, and every kid came out of it with a set of programs they had zero input on.

Marcus's programs came from his specific situation. His biological father kept canceling plans, which hurt in ways Marcus didn't always have words for, and his brain stored it: "things outside of me cause pain, and there's not much I can do about it."

He was sad about it too, underneath the part that looked like not caring. He was sad that his dad kept choosing something else, and sad that the family he had wasn't the family he wanted. His stepdad arrived with authority Marcus never agreed to, and that got tagged: "Rules that get handed down without your say are worth pushing back on."

Those programs made sense given what had actually happened to him, they came from real experience and real pain, and he didn't design them any more than you designed yours.

One thing this book is not going to do is tell you that what happened to you was no big deal, or that the pain that built these programs wasn't real, or that whatever was hard in your situation wasn't hard.

Some of what shaped these programs was unfair. Some of it hurt. Some of it shouldn't have happened. That's real, and it belongs to your story.

What this book is going to do is show you what you get to work with now, regardless of how it got there. Those are two separate things, and keeping them separate is important: what caused the programs isn't the same question as what you do with them now.

The issue is that your brain keeps using those programs forever unless something makes it stop. It writes them in and runs them permanently, and it goes back to ask, "Are these still working?" about as often as your phone asks if you still want that app you downloaded three years ago and never open, which is to say, it doesn't.

There is one more thing worth knowing here, and we'll get to it properly in the next chapter: around age thirteen, just when all these childhood programs are running at full speed, your brain itself goes through a major hardware upgrade, the actual physical structure of it changes, and that upgrade is designed to push you toward independence and away from the authority of the adults who raised you.

The programs were written for a child, the upgraded hardware arrives for someone who is supposed to be becoming an adult, and those two things happen at the same time without anyone explaining it is a big part of why the teen years feel the way they feel.

* * *

The Toolbox Your Brain Built

By the time you're a teenager, your brain has spent your whole life running experiments and has built up a solid collection of responses, behaviors that worked often enough to get kept, and the specific ones are different for everyone because they depend on what worked in your specific environment, but the categories tend to look pretty familiar.

Some people's go-to is anger. Lol, anger is kind of awesome as a tool, cause it works! It makes people back off, it creates space, it stops the pressure and moves the focus somewhere else fast, and if it worked often enough early on your brain paved that road wide and smooth. The cost, though, is just as real: Anger as a primary program burns through trust and relationships in ways that take a long time to show up and even longer to repair, and the people around you start bracing before you even open your mouth.

Some people's main program is silence, which works completely differently but gets some of the same results, because adults get uncomfortable with silence, they try to fill it, they soften, they negotiate.

Humor redirects, charm disarms, tears soften people up, blame deflects attention, disappearing buys time. Every one of these is a real solution to a real problem that your brain found, tested, and decided was worth keeping.

Belonging is in this category too, and it's one of the most powerful relief signals the adolescent brain knows. The need to be part of a group, to have people who have your back, to belong somewhere. It's biological, not weakness.

Neurons and Narratives

The upgraded brain treats social belonging with the same urgency it treats physical safety, because for most of human history those two things were the same. This is why friend selection matters more during these years than at almost any other point in life, and why it's worth looking at directly.

The brain that finds belonging in a group builds its wiring around whatever that group requires. Not as a decision though, but as pure myelination. Whatever behaviors the group runs, the explanations the group uses, the way the group handles conflict and loyalty and accountability, all of it gets practiced and insulated and reinforced. A group that operates on respect and follow-through builds roads that support and reward those behaviors. A group that operates on deflection, on proving loyalty through bad decisions, on belonging being contingent on going along, builds those roads instead, and builds them fast, during the exact window when the wiring is most plastic and most permanent.

The brain that joins a gang isn't running different logic from any other brain. It's running the same logic, finding the fastest available path to belonging and status and relief, and the myelination it's doing in that environment is deep and goes in one direction. You don't have to be in a gang for this to apply. Friend groups do the same work at different intensities.

The question worth asking is: What does this group require of me, and is that what I want my brain to be building?

We want to use that first superpower and send ourselves forward in time. "If I join this group, where will that take me?" but that is also difficult for the teen brain because it downplays harm to self during this phase of development. So instead you can ask weird questions that might sort of shock the brain into a different conclusion.

For example:

- How many old successful gang members are there?
- How many drug dealers reach retirement?
- Who would be the best friend I could choose, if my goal was to get shot and killed?

Strange questions can't be answered by a program that doesn't exist, so they force your brain to think about the answers.

So your brain is full of solutions, actual solutions that your brain found for various reasons, then tested them against actual problems, and refined over years of real experience, and the fact that some of them are causing trouble now just means the situation changed and the programs didn't update with it. You got all brand new hardware, but you are running outdated software on it.

Think about a truck built specifically for driving off-road: big tires, high clearance, handles mud and rocks and rough terrain without breaking a sweat. Drive that same truck on a smooth highway at seventy miles an hour every day and it becomes uncomfortable, inefficient, harder to handle than it needs to be. The truck is performing exactly as designed, the road just changed.

Your programs work the same way, they were designed for the terrain you were in when your brain first built them, some of you were in rough terrain and the programs that got built are heavy-duty for good reason, either way they are performing exactly as designed. The question is whether those are still the right programs for the road you're on now.

Most people arrive in their teen years carrying programs that were designed to work in one very specific environment: that house, that family, with those particular adults, under those specific conditions. Then adolescence happens and suddenly you're in classrooms and friend groups and situations where none of those original conditions apply. The programs have no idea yet, they just keep running until something forces a change.

* * *

What This Looks Like in Real Life

Let's go back to Marcus, because this is exactly what was happening with him whether he knew it or not.

His main program was deflection, which meant that anything that went wrong had an explanation, and that explanation always lived somewhere outside of him, the teacher was unfair, the stepdad was out of line, his mom never listened, his dad kept letting him down, and Marcus had real pieces of real experience behind all of these, which is what made the program so effective, because it was never completely wrong.

Every time something went wrong and Marcus found the outside explanation, the uncomfortable feeling stopped, the chest loosened up, the threat passed, and that result got stored: this works. Every time it worked the road got a little wider, a little faster, a little more automatic, until by ninth grade Marcus didn't experience deflection as a response at all, it was just how things obviously were, his stepdad set a rule and Marcus felt the tightness in his chest and before a single conscious thought happened his brain had already found the outside cause and built the case, his teacher said something and the same thing happened, his dad canceled again, same thing.

The program was so fast and so practiced it had become invisible to him. From the inside, everything looked clear. From the outside, it looked like a kid who refused to look at himself. Both were true at the same time, which is what makes these programs so hard to deal with.

Here's what that looked like for the people around him. Ms. Patterson was a decent teacher, but she also had a program of her own that was kind of broken, and sometimes mislabeled kids too early, before she had enough information to be fair about it. So when she saw a student who *seemed* checked out and had an outside explanation for every grade, her lawyer filed it: "This one isn't interested."

She had thirty-two kids in that class, and her brain, just like everyone else's brain, directed her energy toward the places it seemed likely to have the most impact, so she backed off from Marcus earlier than she should have.

Marcus experienced that as confirmation that she never liked his work. What had really happened is that his program trained her program to stop trying, and then his brain used that result as evidence for the original story. The program created the outcome, then used that same outcome to justify itself, and that's how these things stay locked in long after the situation they were built for is gone.

* * *

When the Program Stops Fitting

Your brain's definition of "works" is narrow to the point of being almost useless for your actual life, because it means one thing: "Did the immediate discomfort stop." The relationship getting worse over time doesn't show up in that measurement, the teacher losing faith in you doesn't register, your stepdad deciding to stop trying doesn't get counted, and your brain just measures the signal it can measure, which is: "Did the chest loosen up, yes or no."

So the program keeps going long after it has stopped producing anything worth having, because from your brain's measurement point it's still technically doing its job, deflecting is still stopping the immediate discomfort, silence is still creating space, anger is still moving people, the short-term signal keeps arriving, and there's no system in place for tallying what all of that is costing on the other end.

Jordan figured this out the hard way. Jordan's program was silence, the protective kind of stillness that made adults uncomfortable enough to back off, and it worked well when he was young, adults did soften, conflicts did ease up, people did give him space. By ninth grade the same program had a completely different effect, teachers stopped asking questions, friends stopped trying to include him, group projects formed around him rather than with him, and Jordan told himself he liked being alone, which was easier than looking at what the program had really built.

A lot of teens in Jordan's position find their way to social media around this point, and it makes complete sense that they do, because online you can build a version of yourself that people respond to, you can find groups that mirror exactly what you're feeling, and the feedback comes without the vulnerability that actual in-person connection requires. The *relief* is real. We'll come back to what else comes with it.

Except Jordan didn't like being alone, he wanted people to reach out, wanted to feel included, wanted the connection that his program was making impossible without ever announcing it was doing that. When the connection didn't come, his brain handed him a role to explain it: Victim. Nobody reaches out to me, nobody tries, I'm just not the kind of person people include. The program kept people at a distance and then used that distance as evidence that he had every right to stay behind the wall, two loops reinforcing each other, both invisible from inside.

Same rule, same program, same brain doing exactly what it was built to do. Completely different result from what Jordan wanted. The situation changed and the program had no idea.

* * *

Why the Brain Keeps Running the Old Program

Your brain keeps a program as long as it appears to be working. The problem is that your brain is terrible with the word "appears." It measures one signal: discomfort reduced, yes or no, and skips the long-term cost entirely.

So the deflection keeps going because the chest keeps loosening up when it fires. The silence keeps holding because people still back off when it lands. The anger keeps coming because the room still settles.

From your brain's point of view, all of these are still doing their job.

There's also something else going on: your brain starts filtering what you pay attention to in order to protect the program. If your stored rules say that outside forces are the source of problems, your brain starts directing your attention toward evidence that confirms that and away from anything that complicates it. The teacher who was fair doesn't make it into the collection. The stepdad who was trying gets minimized. The program basically protects itself by controlling what counts as data.

This is why two people can be in the exact same situation and walk away with completely different memories of what happened, both certain they have it right. Both brains recorded what they saw accurately. It's just that what they saw got filtered through the program before it ever became a conscious thought.

Two different filters produce two different highlight reels: two people in the same room who could swear they were somewhere completely different.

Your parents run this same equipment, by the way, just as fast and just as automatically as you do. Their programs are filtering their read on you the whole time your programs are filtering your read on them. And when your mom says, "You always do this," her brain has been collecting the times you did this and skipping the times you didn't. And when you say, "She never listens," yours has been doing the same thing in the other direction.

Two programs going full speed, both absolutely convinced they're seeing clearly. That's basically every family argument that has ever happened.

This is also why punishment alone almost never changes behavior in any lasting way, which is worth understanding because it affects a lot of your daily life. The adults in your world are mostly operating on a pretty simple theory: "If something costs you enough you'll stop doing it."

This sounds logical, but logic is the last language your nervous system speaks.

What really happens in a punishment situation is that the behavior produces an immediate result first. The room goes still, the pressure lifts, the tension moves somewhere else, and that result lands in your nervous system before the consequence ever arrives. So by the time the consequence shows up, your brain has already stored the reward. You get both, and your brain keeps the behavior because the relief came first and felt more real than whatever came after.

That's why you can end up in the same kind of trouble over and over and have no idea why you keep going there, because from the inside your nervous system is just running the program that produced relief, and the punishment keeps using the wrong language to change anything.

* * *

What You're Working With

You are carrying programs that were written for a situation that probably looks nothing like your life right now. Some of them are still serving you well, and some of them are costing you things you can't see from the inside because the cost is delayed and the program is good at explaining the delay away. Your brain is running all of them the same way regardless.

That's just what brains do. They run what they were given, and they keep only what worked.

The part that changes things is knowing that. When these programs feel like personality, like just who you are, like obvious truth about how the world works, that feeling is real to you. It's also the program talking.

The minute you can see a program as a program instead of as reality, something opens up. You can look at it. You can ask if this thing you are doing is still working for the situations you're in now.

Then you can, with enough repetition, start building roads that go somewhere better.

It's gonna to take a little longer than you would like, and it requires more patience than a lot of people expect. Rewiring means repeating something new often enough that your brain starts investing in it. It also means giving the people around you enough consistent evidence of the new behavior so that their programs start updating their read on you. And those two things together take real time.

We are going to come back to exactly how that process works later in this book. If your parents are reading the parent version of this book somewhere, they are getting the same information from a different angle, because this goes both directions.

For now, the thing worth taking out of this chapter is simpler than any of that.

You are running programs you didn't write. Knowing that is the beginning of getting to write your own.

* * *

Marcus, One More Time

Marcus was still running his program at the end of ninth grade, and from inside it everything looked fine. His stepdad had backed off, his teachers had mostly stopped pushing, his friends agreed with him or said nothing, and his brain kept collecting all of that as evidence that his read on things was correct.

Nobody changes anything that is working, or at least nothing they "think" is working, which to the brain is the same thing.

Something was happening underneath the surface though, something small and slow and completely unremarkable, which is exactly how the most important things tend to happen. The world was getting a little smaller every semester in ways he couldn't point to, just in the way that certain conversations stopped happening and certain doors stopped opening and certain people stopped showing up.

Underneath the deflection and the case-building and the way everything had an outside explanation, Marcus was sometimes just sad about it—sad that things kept going the way they went, sad that the family he had wasn't the one he'd wanted.

The program gave him a place to file that, but it didn't make the feeling go away.

The program was doing exactly what it was built to do, it just wasn't enough anymore.

In Chapter Four we're going to look at what happens when the strategies start visibly failing, when the cost gets impossible to ignore. Before we get there, something else happened to Marcus around age thirteen that changed the whole equation, remember right about then his brain got upgraded, and nobody told him what that meant.

* * *

Next: The Upgrade Nobody Explained

CHAPTER THREE

The Upgrade Nobody Explained

What happened at twelve or thirteen, why defiance is biological, and why nobody told you any of this

Something changed. You probably noticed it before anyone put words to it. The rules started feeling heavier, adults started feeling more irritating, a kind of restlessness showed up that hadn't been there before, and the strangest part was that nothing obvious had happened to cause any of it. No big event, no visible turning point, just one day the world felt a little different and you didn't know why.

If nobody explained it to you, you probably did what most people do, you made a story about it. Maybe the story was that you were finally seeing things clearly: that the adults around you had always been this way and you were just now smart enough to notice. Maybe the story was that something was wrong with you: that you had become difficult, angry, hard to be around, and you weren't sure where that came from. Maybe both of those stories were running at the same time.

Here's what was happening: your brain was being renovated, the physical structure of your brain was changing in ways that rewired how you processed authority, identity, emotion, and risk, and it happened on a schedule that had nothing to do with what was going on in your life or how ready you were for it.

* * *

What the Upgrade Is

Around age twelve or thirteen, sometimes a little earlier for girls and a little later for boys, your brain goes through one of the most significant structural changes of your entire life. This isn't puberty, though puberty is happening around the same time. This is something different happening inside the brain itself; a massive reorganization of how it's wired and what it prioritizes.

Here's the short version of what's going on. The limbic system, which is the part of your brain that handles emotion, status, social connection, risk, and reward, gets a significant upgrade in power and sensitivity. It becomes louder, faster, and more influential over your behavior. At the same time, the prefrontal cortex, which is the part responsible for consequences, long-term thinking, impulse control, and weighing decisions, develops much more slowly, and won't finish developing until you're in your mid-twenties.

So at twelve or thirteen you are handed a significantly more powerful emotional engine, and the brakes are still being installed.

That's the upgrade. Powerful engine, brakes in progress, no manual, and nobody at the door to explain any of it.

This is also why cannabis is a specific risk during these years in a way it isn't for adults. THC directly disrupts prefrontal cortex development. The prefrontal cortex is already the weakest link in the upgraded brain, the part running furthest behind, the brakes that are still being installed. Regular cannabis use during adolescence doesn't just get you high. It interferes with the development of the exact structure that handles consequences, impulse control, and long-term thinking, and it does so during this window when that structure is most actively being built.

Research is consistent on this: Adolescent cannabis use is associated with measurable, lasting reductions in the very functions the teen brain needs most to develop. The risks are simply not the same for a fully developed adult brain. They are much more dangerous during this phase, because the construction is happening now.

There's also something called synaptic pruning happening at the same time, which sounds more alarming than it is. Your brain has an enormous number of neural connections built up from childhood, way more than it needs, and while it has been cutting back for a long time, adolescence is when it starts cutting even more of the ones it doesn't use and strengthening the ones it does. Your brain is essentially deciding what to keep and what to trim, and it makes those decisions based on what's been getting used. The childhood connections that haven't been exercised start getting pruned away, and the pathways you keep using, including the childhood programs you have already been running, get reinforced. The brain is literally reshaping itself around the habits you've either already built, or are consciously building now.

This is also why adolescence is such a critical window. The pruning and reinforcement that happens in these years is building the neural architecture you're going to carry into adulthood, and it's doing it while the emotional system is running loudest and the judgment system is the most behind. That combination is not a mistake. It is designed by evolution, but it does create some very predictable and very confusing experiences.

* * *

Why Defiance Is the Upgrade Working Correctly

This one is worth reading twice: The impulse to push back against authority that shows up at this age is the upgrade doing *exactly what it's supposed to do*.

It's not a malfunction. It's not you becoming a worse person. It's your brain running a biological program that has been part of human development for a very long time, and it's doing it on purpose.

Think about what adolescence is preparing you for. At some point you have to leave, you have to be able to function independently, make your own decisions, evaluate authority rather than just obey it, and trust your own judgment even when the people around you disagree. A brain that remained completely deferential to adults forever would produce an adult who couldn't function without being told what to do. So the brain, right on schedule, starts testing the authority structure it's been operating inside. It starts asking:

- "Is this worth following?"
- "Does this person know what they're talking about?"
- "Is this rule legitimate or just a habit?"
- "Do I have to accept this?"

Those are good questions. Those are the questions of someone who is preparing for independence. The problem is that they arrive at twelve or thirteen, when you don't yet have the judgment, the experience, or the emotional regulation to run them well. So they come out as arguments, eye-rolls, slammed doors, and the particular kind of certainty that only teenagers and very old people have where you just know you're right about everything.

The defiance is also, underneath the frustration it causes, a way your brain is testing whether the relationships in your life are strong enough to handle disagreement. Strong relationships are ones that can hold conflict without breaking, and your brain is preparing you to be an adult who can have those kinds of relationships.

It just doesn't tell you that's what it's doing. It just makes authority feel insulting and makes you want to push back, and you have to figure out the rest yourself.

Marcus was doing this. Every time his stepdad made a rule, his brain wasn't just processing the rule, it was processing the legitimacy of the source ("Bro you ain't my dad"). And since his brain had already decided that authority imposed without consent was worth pushing back on, the upgrade gave that existing program a lot more fuel.

What looked from the outside like a kid being difficult was, from the inside, a perfectly logical biological process running on top of a program that had been building for years. Neither the defiance nor the program was random. Both made complete sense given everything that had come before.

* * *

Why Everything Feels Personal Now

Before the upgrade, correction was pretty simple, it meant something specific happened that needed to change. After the upgrade, the limbic system starts running a filter over almost everything that gets said to you, and that filter has one question: what does this say about me?

So when a teacher says "redo this," the upgraded brain might hear something more like "you aren't good enough." And when a parent says "clean your room," the upgraded brain could translate that into, "I don't trust you." And when someone looks at you a certain way in the hallway your brain can turn that into a whole other story about what that person thinks about you before you've even processed what their face was doing.

The original input and the meaning your brain assigns can be completely different things, and this happens fast, faster than thinking, before you have any chance to check the translation.

This is because the limbic system, now louder and faster than before, has added status to the list of things it treats like survival. Before adolescence, the brain's survival concerns are pretty concrete:

- Am I physically safe?
- Am I part of the group?
- Do I have what I need?

After the upgrade, status and identity get added to that list with the same weight:

- Am I respected?
- Do I matter?
- Am I being seen as capable?
- Do I have any control over my own life?

Those questions start registering as urgent in the same way that cold and hunger registered as urgent when you were a baby, and when the answer seems to be no, the response is just as immediate.

This is why correction feels sharp in a way it didn't before, why a calm parent can still feel threatening, and why being wrong in front of people registers as something closer to physical pain than it used to. It's also why you might notice yourself exhausted in ways that are hard to explain, because your nervous system is now running the status scan constantly, through every conversation, every look, every tone of voice, checking and rechecking whether you're okay, and that takes a lot of energy.

* * *

Why Your Parents Are Running Outdated Software

Here is something your parents probably don't know about themselves: most of them stopped updating their parenting model around the time you were maybe eight or nine but definitely around ten.

That was the last major recalibration, the point where they figured out what worked with you. They've mostly been running that version since, because it was working and there was no obvious reason to change it.

Then the upgrade hit you at twelve or thirteen, and suddenly the version that worked on the nine-year-old you was running on a brain that had been fundamentally restructured, and it fit about as well as a childhood program fits the situations it was never designed for. The rules were the same, the tone was the same, the expectation was the same, but everything about how you received and processed those things had changed, and your parents often had no idea why it stopped working.

From their side, it can feel like you changed overnight and became someone they don't recognize, and that's accurate. You did change. The brain changed. The upgrade happened. The person they'd been parenting for a decade is now running different hardware.

From your side, it can feel like they're treating you like a child even though you're clearly not a child anymore, and that's also accurate, because the version of you they have programmed in was a child and they haven't updated the software. They need to load "Adolescent 5.0" instead of running on "Child 3.11."

So you both got caught in a gap that neither of you created and neither of you was warned about. Your brain upgraded on its biological schedule without asking for permission and without sending a notification. Your parents kept running what worked because nothing told them to update. Two programs, both reasonable given the information each side had, completely out of sync with each other, and every argument that followed was partly just those two programs running into each other.

The parents who handle this best are the ones who figure out, usually through some painful trial and error, that the upgrade requires them to change their approach. They negotiate more and command less, to explain reasoning rather than just invoking authority, to treat the defiance as information rather than disrespect. Most parents don't get there without a fight. Some never get there at all. That's not necessarily bad parenting, it's just that nobody told them about the upgrade either.

* * *

There Used to Be a Test!

Go back a few thousand or even just several hundred years to basically any traditional culture you can name, and you'll find something that our culture stopped doing, and we really don't know why. There used to be a formal transition ritual at adolescence.

Most of these happened right around thirteen, and they varied enormously in their specifics, but they shared a basic structure. The young person went through something difficult, something that required real capability, and at the end of it they were formally recognized as having crossed a threshold. Before the ritual, you were a child, after it you were an adult, and everyone in the community updated their relationship with you accordingly.

The point wasn't just ceremony. The test was doing something functional: it was giving the brain's new defiance and independence drive somewhere legitimate to land. Instead of pushing back against parents for years in an undefined struggle with no clear endpoint, you went through something hard, demonstrated that you could handle it, and the community acknowledged the upgrade. The brain got the signal it was biologically looking for, that the questions of capability and worth had been answered, and everyone could move forward.

We don't have that anymore. What we have instead is a very long, very undefined middle period that can last anywhere from five to fifteen years, depending on how things go. In that period, you're biologically an adult but socially still treated as a developing child. The drive for independence is fully activated, but the legitimate pathway to it is unclear, and nobody announces when or how the transition is supposed to happen.

The upgrade arrives on schedule. The test is missing. And the brain, which was built expecting to run the independence drive through a structured challenge and come out the other side, just keeps running it indefinitely instead.

Think about it, kids used to know everything they were going to have to understand and knew every skill they had to develop for the test, and they knew it all through childhood. So they had time to prepare for the test.

Society since then, just bailed on the test, and kids today have no idea what the skills and understanding required to perform as an adult even are, until you start looking for that information, right about the time you would historically be testing for it.

That's not your fault. It's your problem though, and it's worth understanding, because a lot of the chaos of the teen years isn't random. It's a brain that got the upgrade and is looking for the test and can't find it, so it starts generating its own, usually in ways that are inconvenient for everyone involved.

* * *

The Upgrade Runs Differently Depending on Who You Are

The upgrade doesn't hit everyone the same way, and the most consistent difference is between how it tends to run for girls versus how it tends to run for boys, and it's worth laying this out plainly because a lot of confusion and a lot of unfair comparisons come from not knowing it.

For girls, the limbic system upgrade tends to happen earlier, sometimes starting around ten or eleven, and it hits harder in terms of emotional intensity and social sensitivity. Girls going through the upgrade are often dealing with significantly amplified emotional experiences and a very sharp awareness of social dynamics, inclusion and exclusion, reputation and relationships, at an age when they have even less developed judgment than they will a couple of years later. The emotional experience can be overwhelming in ways that are hard to explain to adults who have forgotten what it felt like, and the social stakes feel enormous because to the upgraded limbic system, they *are*.

For boys, the upgrade tends to come later, and the prefrontal cortex development that handles judgment and impulse control tends to lag behind even further, which means the gap between emotional power and the ability to regulate it is often wider and lasts longer. Risk-taking goes up, sensitivity to shame and status in peer groups goes up, the drive to establish independence from parental authority goes up, and the tools to navigate any of that skillfully are still seriously behind. The behavior that results often looks like recklessness or aggression or just general lack of sense, and some of it is, but a lot of it is just the upgrade running without adequate brakes.

Neither version is better or worse, they're just different timelines running through the same basic renovation, and understanding this matters because a lot of people spend years comparing themselves to peers who are at different points in the process and drawing conclusions about their own capability or worth based on comparisons that were never fair in the first place. You are on your own timeline. The upgrade runs when it runs.

* * *

Marcus, Mid-Upgrade

By the time Marcus was thirteen, the upgrade was well underway, and he had no idea that's what was happening, he just knew that everything felt more urgent and more personal than it used to, that his stepdad's authority felt more intolerable than it had a year before, and that the restlessness that had been building in him didn't seem to have a name or a clear cause.

His stepdad was still running the version of parenting that had been designed for a younger Marcus, issuing rules and expecting compliance while not offering much in the way of reasoning, because that's what had worked before. The upgraded Marcus, whose brain was now biologically programmed to test authority, found every one of those rules more aggravating than the last, and every time he pushed back and his stepdad held firm without explanation, his brain filed it as more evidence that the authority was illegitimate and worth resisting. Each and every time, stepdad was just more of a jerk.

What neither of them could see was that they were both responding reasonably to the situation as they understood it. Marcus's brain was doing exactly what brains do at thirteen, testing the authority structure, looking for reasoning, and pushing for some acknowledgment that he was no longer the eight-year-old the rules had been written for. His stepdad was doing what parents do when a kid who used to be manageable starts being difficult. They start holding firmer, adding more rules, trying to reassert the structure that used to work. Two reasonable responses to incomplete information, each making the other worse.

The sadness underneath all of it was still there too, the sadness about his dad, about the family situation, about things not being what he wanted them to be, and the upgrade had made that sadder and louder without giving him better tools to hold it. The deflection program his brain had built years earlier to manage pain he couldn't control now had a much more powerful emotional engine running it. The arguments got bigger, the distance grew, and his world kept getting smaller in ways nobody was tracking.

Nobody had explained the upgrade to Marcus, and nobody had explained it to his stepdad. So neither of them knew that what looked like a character problem was mostly a biology problem. The friction between them was partly just two sets of outdated software running into a brain that had been upgraded without warning. If someone had, it probably wouldn't have fixed everything, but it might have changed how they interpreted each other, and that would have changed something.

* * *

What You're Dealing With

So here is the diagnosis, stated plainly: You are mid-upgrade.

The emotional system got the new hardware first> The judgment and regulation system is still catching up. You are navigating that gap in an environment that mostly wasn't designed with the gap in mind, around adults who weren't told about the gap, using programs that were built in childhood for a completely different situation and are now running on significantly more powerful hardware than they were designed for.

The defiance you feel is biological and correct. It's your brain preparing you for independence and testing whether the authority structures around you are worth engaging with. The intensity of everything, the way correction feels personal, the way status feels like survival, the way small things carry enormous weight, that's the limbic system running louder than the regulation system, doing its job, exactly as designed. The chaos in the relationship with your parents is partly just two different software versions trying to run at the same time without a manual.

None of this means you don't have to figure it out. It's not your fault, but still your problem, remember?

The upgrade doesn't excuse the behavior it produces. The missing test is still missing whether or not that's fair. The childhood programs your brain built before any of this are going to keep running until something changes them. T people around you are going to keep responding to your behavior rather than your biology. Understanding what's happening is the beginning of being able to do something about it, but it's not a substitute for actually doing something.

What you're dealing with is real> It's harder than most adults remember, and it is survivable…more than survivable. The upgrade is exactly what it sounds like: your brain is becoming more capable, more powerful, more your own, and the chaos of the process is the cost of that, not evidence that something went wrong.

You are not broken. You are mid-upgrade. Those are completely different things, and the rest of this book is about what you do with that.

* * *

Next: When the Strategies Start Failing

CHAPTER FOUR

When the Strategies Start Failing

The cost that arrived without an announcement, and the gap that changes everything

Marcus still had his phone in his hand when he noticed the text wasn't coming. Forty minutes, which wouldn't be that unusual, except this was a friend who used to respond before you finished putting your phone down. Something about the waiting felt different from regular waiting, and Marcus sat there and felt the familiar tightness starting in his chest, except this time the thing that usually kicked in to explain it away was slower than usual, working harder than it used to for something it used to produce automatically.

He put the phone down and went and did something else. The program caught up eventually and handed him an explanation and once again he moved on. But for about thirty seconds, *something had been different*, a small lag between the thing that happened and the story that usually arrived to cover it, and in that lag was something he hadn't felt in a long time: the situation, uninterpreted.

This chapter is about that thirty seconds.

How a Strategy Expires

Think about a tool designed for a specific job. It handles everything the job throws at it, produces exactly the result it was built to produce, and works every time under the conditions it was made for. Move it to a different environment, different materials, different pressure, and it keeps running the same sequence it always has, except now the environment is different and the result starts coming out wrong. The tool has no way to register that, it just keeps going.

The childhood wiring your brain built was designed for specific conditions, specific people, specific rules, specific kinds of pressure, and the responses that worked in that environment worked because those conditions held. When the conditions change, the wiring doesn't update. It just keeps firing the same sequence. The gap between what it was built for and what the current situation requires gets wider, slowly, across months and sometimes years, until the program stops producing what it was designed to produce.

This doesn't happen all at once. It happens in an accumulation of small data points your brain mostly ignores: a teacher who used to accept the excuse now marks it down without comment, the friend who used to absorb the deflection now pulls back in a way that reads differently, an adult who used to argue now just handles the situation and leaves. Each of these is new information the program could use to update itself, but it *doesn't*, because the program isn't running a cost-benefit analysis. It's running toward relief, and relief is still showing up often enough to keep the road paved.

The expiration becomes visible when the relief stops coming, or shows up in tiny amounts, for a shorter time, and just does not work anymore. Or the cost that has been stacking in the background becomes too big to explain. That's the moment. It's usually the first real opening you get a chance to look at it, because up until that point the program was doing its job of keeping the discomfort managed, or at least well enough that looking wasn't necessary.

* * *

The Fine Print Nobody Read

When your brain writes a program, it's essentially signing a contract on your behalf. The big print is easy to read: "This behavior will reduce the discomfort you're feeling right now."

That part your brain understood immediately, locked it in, and started running it. The fine print is the part nobody reads. The same way you don't read the terms at the bottom of a new app before you tap agree, you just tap agree because you want the thing, and the terms seem like something you can deal with later.

The fine print on every one of these programs is the same: There might be costs for this program and they will accumulate in the background.

These costs will feel like they're just happening to you, and the connection between the behavior and the cost will be invisible enough that your brain will find other explanations before it points at the deal.

That's what the accumulation looks like in real life:

- Teachers who used to give you some benefit of the doubt just stop
- Friends who used to reach out start letting you come to them
- Trust that used to be offered has to be earned instead
- Adults who used to push back on you start managing you instead

It sounds easier, but means something different. None of these arrive with a flashing sign that says, "You did this to yourself, stop deflecting already!"

There is no arrow pointing at the source, and no notice that the costs have been hiding somewhere. They just arrive, and your brain, which is very good at protecting itself, assigns outside explanations:

- Meh, that teacher was never that engaged

- Those friends are unreliable
- Those adults are just tired

The connection between your behavior and the cost stays invisible, and your brain keeps it that way.

Here's the part that makes this stickier than it sounds. Your brain has a built-in threat scanner that runs constantly in the background. When something happens, it doesn't actually analyze the situation fresh. It does something faster and lazier: it checks what it already has on file and asks one question, "Seen this before?"

If yes, it labels it **Familiar**. Then if Familiar, it's no threat, so a different part of your brain basically says "Nah bro, we good" and stands the stress response down. The body relaxes. Everything feels normal. And here's the problem: when your body feels normal, your brain takes that as *confirmation* that the story is true. So the outside explanations your brain already assigned like teacher not engaged, friends unreliable, and adults tired, gets scanned, and come back as familiar. Your body stays calm and the story doesn't even need to be defended. It just gets stamped as fact every time and you never made a single decision about any of it.

The contract comes due when the cost gets large enough so that even outside explanations require more effort than the relief is worth. That's usually when something cracks.

Why the Lectures Didn't Work

If people who cared about you pointed at the problem before it expired, you probably knew what they were saying. You might have even agreed at that time. But the program kept running anyway, and if you're being honest with yourself, that probably wasn't the first time that cycle completed.

A lot of teenagers decide that means something about who they are when it really just means something about how behavior change works. Your brain doesn't reorganize because of information, it reorganizes when the comfort collapses. So, as long as the program is producing relief, it has more pull on your behavior than any conversation can, because the conversation is happening in words, and the program is happening in your body. It's physical and immediate. Your nervous system has been speaking body language since before you had words. Logic and lectures talk about the future, but the program lives now.

The brain always listens to what's right in front of it first.

A program doesn't expire because someone describes its cost convincingly. It expires when the relief it was built to produce stops being worth what it's taking.

Of course none of this means the people trying to reach you were wrong. It means they were speaking a language your nervous system wasn't equipped to act on yet. If lectures could rewire behavior, every parent on earth would be the best parent who ever lived, and every kid who reached the teen years would have zero trouble and go on to be incredibly successful, because parents give lectures constantly and they mean every word. We just can't get there that way, brains don't work like that. The entry point for change isn't understanding, it's feeling something you can't hand off to the program. Something that you can't explain away with a story.

* * *

What the Cost Looks Like

The real cost doesn't come screaming in with a loud boom. It doesn't come in the form of a confrontation or a consequence or a threshold you can point to. It usually comes in the form of absence, and people are not very good at noticing what isn't there, or asking why it stopped showing up.

It looks like a teacher who used to give you a look that meant something now writing your name in the grade book and moving on. It looks like the friend group that formed a plan that didn't include you, not out of cruelty, but just because that happens when someone has been unreliable often enough that people stop expecting reliability. It looks like adults who used to push back on you, which felt bad but kind of implied trust and had meaning, now just process you through whatever system handles the situation. That feels like you are not part of it, like they just "handle" you. Conflict means you're still in the equation. Being processed means the equation changed, and what changed is that you moved from someone worth investing in, to someone who needs managing, and those are two completely different categories. Worth investing in means someone believes the effort has a return. Being managed means they think putting in effort isn't worth it.

The absence doesn't argue, because there's nothing there to argue with, just the space where something used to be, and you can build a case against someone who pushes back but you can't build a case against a teacher who just moves on without a look. The friends are busy, the teacher has thirty other kids, the adults are tired, and all of those explanations can be true and still be doing the work of keeping you from asking the more useful question: What behavior of yours might be causing this?

There's also something worth naming about the difference between absence and freedom, because from the outside they can look identical. When adults stop pushing back on you, when teachers stop correcting you, when people stop expecting things from you, there's a version of that which feels like relief, like finally having some breathing room. That feeling is real, but we want to look at that carefully and directly, because there are two completely different reasons people stop pushing back on you. One is that they trust you enough to give you space, and the other is that they've decided the effort just isn't worth it. The first one is like being left alone is something you earn. The second one is like something that happens to you, and the difference between them is not always obvious from inside the program that's handing you the answers.

Most teenagers experiencing the second kind believe they're experiencing the first, because the program is very good at that particular translation. The relief that comes from not being corrected feels like the relief that comes from being trusted, and your brain doesn't distinguish between them, it just logs the relief. The cost of that confusion is that you can spend a long time believing people backed off because they trust you, when they actually backed off because they stopped trying, and not know the difference until something you needed was already gone.

* * *

Marcus at the Moment

By the second half of ninth grade, Marcus's world had gotten small enough that even his brain was having trouble keeping up with the maintenance. His stepdad had stopped arguing, started issuing rules, and leaving the room. His mom had taken on "the tone" with him, the kind that means someone is managing the relationship rather than being in it. Ms. Patterson had moved her energy elsewhere a long time ago. A few of the friendships that felt solid had thinned in ways he couldn't account for, guys who used to answer immediately were slower, plans that used to form easily required more effort, and twice in one month he found out something had happened without him.

Neurons and Narratives

The program was handling all of it. Every piece of evidence went through the filter and came out with an outside address, stepdad's control issues, mom's anxiety, the teacher's preferences, and his friends' flakiness. The lawyer was still building cases, and every new explanation went through the threat scanner, came back familiar, got cleared, and the story got a little more solid every time. But the caseload had become heavy, and somewhere underneath the case-building was a whisper, an awareness that the explanations were requiring more work than they used to, that the situations were stacking faster than the explanations could process them, and that every explanation, when you lined them all up, was pointing in the same direction without any of them landing on him.

The Thursday afternoon with the phone wasn't a revelation. It was a lag. The program loaded, but it loaded slower, and in those thirty seconds it took to catch up, Marcus felt the situation the way it was before the story arrived to cover it. A friend who used to be right there, was suddenly not right there, and no slick answer from the lawyer was helping.

Marcus kept going, a program eventually offered a little relief. But something had come loose that hadn't been loose before: a small gap between what happened and what the program told him it meant. Underneath the deflection and the case-building and the way every situation had an address that wasn't him, Marcus was sometimes just sad about it. He was sad that things kept going the way they went, sad that the family he had wasn't the one he'd wanted, sad in a way the program hadn't figured out how to file yet. He hadn't told anyone. But it was there.

* * *

Why the Program Defends Itself

Even when a program is clearly costing you, the brain keeps running it. It doesn't feel like stubbornness from the inside, it feels normal. It feels like you're simply seeing the situation accurately and everyone else is wrong about what's causing it.

Two things keep this going. The first is that the program is still producing some relief, even when the net result is negative. The deflection still loosens the chest a little, the anger still creates space, the silence still buys some distance, and the brain is measuring that signal, not the spreadsheet of what it's costing across the year. It doesn't stop running a tool because the tool is running up debt it can't see. It stops when the tool stops producing what it was built to produce.

Think about how that works in a real situation. Someone who uses anger as their main program gets into a conflict. The anger fires, the room goes tense, people back off, the pressure lifts, and the brain logs it: this worked. The fact that the relationship lost something in those thirty seconds, that the other person is now a little more guarded, a little less likely to try again, and that trust moved in a direction that's going to take a lot of consistent behavior to reverse, none of that registers in the right place. The brain felt the pressure drop, and so logged the result. The fact that something else was also happening, something the brain wasn't measuring, never makes it into the file.

The second thing is that after enough repetition, the program stops being something you do and becomes something you are. The deflection doesn't feel like a strategy you picked up somewhere, it feels like your honest read on situations. The anger doesn't feel like a tool your brain paved a road to, it feels like a reasonable response to unreasonable things. The silence doesn't feel like an avoidance strategy, it feels like who you are with people. Changing who you are feels completely different from changing what you do, it feels like losing something, which is why the brain defends the program even when the evidence against it is stacking up in plain sight.

This is also why real loss breaks through in a way that logic doesn't. When something you care about starts going away, the program has no filing system for it. It can explain away a teacher. It can explain away a grade. It has a much harder time explaining away a friend becoming someone who used to text back immediately, but no longer does.

* * *

The Gap

When the program lags, there's a moment, and honestly it's not always thirty seconds. Sometimes it's just a little longer than a second, sometimes shorter, where the situation exists before the story covers it. That moment is the gap.

It doesn't feel like an opportunity. It feels like the particular discomfort of having your usual explanations unavailable, like reaching for something that's always been there and finding the shelf empty, and the instinct is to close it as fast as possible, either by running the program harder or by finding a new explanation that does the same job.

Both of those options close the gap. That's why most people close it. The gap is uncomfortable, the program is fast, and comfort is immediate. Staying in the gap requires something the program was specifically built to prevent: holding the feeling long enough to let it tell you something before you resolve it.

That's harder than it sounds cause the program moves fast and your brain has years of practice closing it before you notice it opened. The gap is the space where the wiring doesn't have an answer ready, and a brain that has been running efficient programs since before you could talk isn't set up to hold that space. It feels like exposure, like standing somewhere with no cover while you wait for something you can't name.

Which is exactly why it matters. The gap is uncomfortable because the program isn't running, and the program isn't running because the situation has outrun it, and the situation has outrun it because something real is happening that the program wasn't built to handle. All of that is information. The discomfort isn't a problem to fix. It's the feeling of the honest situation landing before the story covers it, and if you can feel that and just chill long enough to ask the right question, that's where everything changes.

The honest question isn't the comfortable one, the one the program would ask: why does this keep happening to me? It's the one that points at something you can influence: what does my wiring have to do with this result? Some things are other people's fault. Some situations are unfair. None of that changes by asking the honest question. What changes is that you find the part of the situation that belongs to you, the only part you have any real leverage over, the part that's been accumulating cost in the background while the fine print did its work.

Your brain built what it built from real experiences, with real logic, and it built it before you had any say in the design. The program isn't a character flaw. It's wiring that was built for conditions that have changed, running in conditions it wasn't built for, collecting a cost that's been invisible because the program was covering for it. The gap is where you find out what's been happening.

Marcus on a Thursday afternoon, phone in hand, thirty seconds of lag before the program loaded, was in the gap. He didn't know what to do with it yet, didn't have a name for it, closed it, and moved on. But something had come loose, and what comes loose is what the rest of this book is about.

* * *

Next: What Creates Change

CHAPTER FIVE

Responsibility and Integrity

The cheat code your parents can't say no to, and why your word is the only currency that compounds

Marcus figured it out on a Tuesday in October.

Keep in mind he wasn't trying to figure anything out, he was just tired of being in trouble. His stepdad had added another rule that week, something about checking in before making plans, and it was one more rule on top of the ones already there. Marcus was in top form, running that usual program, building a case, getting ready to hammer back. Then he stopped for a second and did a little time travel. He knew what the whole argument would sound like, and he knew how he would feel, and he knew it would change absolutely nothing, so he thought about it instead, looking for a new strategy.

His stepdad added rules every time something happened he couldn't predict. Marcus went out without checking in, so now there was a check-in rule. Marcus was late twice in a month, so now there was a new curfew. Every new rule was a direct response to a specific thing Marcus had done or hadn't done. Which meant, if Marcus was right, that the rules were basically a map of the ways his stepdad didn't trust him yet.

The part that hit a little differently than Marcus expected: nobody had taught his stepdad to stop trusting him. *Marcus had.* Stepdad might have been the one setting the rules, but he wasn't the one making them… *Marcus was.*

He didn't say any of this out loud. He turned it over in his mind for a few minutes, which was a few minutes longer than he usually spent on anything that had his own name on it. Then he went and did his homework.

Nothing changed that day. Something started.

* * *

The Thing Your Parents Can't Say No To

This is going to sound so simple that your first instinct will be to blow it off. Try not to do that, because the reason it sounds simple is that it *works*, and things that work often look obvious once someone says them out loud.

Adults, specifically the adults who have authority over your life right now, aren't primarily interested in controlling you. It's more like managing risk. Every rule, every curfew, every check-in requirement, every time they say no to something you wanted, they are trying to predict what happens next.

The adults who are easiest on teenagers are not the nicest ones, they're the ones who have built up enough reliable data on that specific teenager that the risk calculation keeps coming back low. Trust isn't a feeling, it's a prediction-based history. That applies to everyone all the time. When adults trust you, what they're saying is "based on your track record, I can predict what you'll do, and I'm comfortable with what I predict."

This means the lever that moves everything, the one that works every single time on every adult in any situation, is demonstrable reliability. Promises won't get you there, and everyone knows how far arguments tend to go. Being charming is a real skill and worth having, but it won't change the calculation. Being good at the conversation is a real asset, but it also won't move this particular number. Doing what you said you would do, when you said you would do it, often enough that their prediction about you changes. That's the thing.

When that happens, something automatic follows. Adults can't help it. The brain that built a prediction around you and kept finding the prediction confirmed starts updating the risk calculation downward, and rules that existed because the risk calculation was high start looking unnecessary. Your parents aren't going to sit down and formally decide to give you more freedom. They are going to notice, without quite being able to explain why, that they're less worried, and the rules are going to loosen in the same way they got tight, gradually, without anybody saying that's what would happen.

That's the cheat code. Your parents can't say no to it because it doesn't leave them anything to say no to. You don't ask for freedom, you produce the evidence and let their brains do the rest. Which means you are now the one doing the programming. The repetition of reliable behavior will produce new responses *in them*, and will force their brains to develop new programs of their own. Same mechanism, your hands on the controls this time.

* * *

How Trust Transfers Into Freedom

So while your brain is telling you that you deserve freedom, and your defiance is telling you to demand it, and you will argue that if they give you the freedom you should already have you can prove you deserve it. But that's backwards. Sure, it makes sense emotionally but produces the opposite of the intended result. Asking for or demanding freedom before establishing reliability reads to the adult's brain as exactly the thing they were already worried about, someone who wants the expanded space without having built the foundation that makes the space safe to give. The more you push for freedom you haven't yet demonstrated you can handle, the tighter the rules get, and the more you push back against the tighter rules, the more data the adult collects that confirms they were right to be cautious.

The sequence that works runs the other way. You produce reliability first. Do this in small, specific, observable ways, consistently enough that the adult's prediction about you changes before you ask for anything. Then when you ask, the ask lands in a completely different environment. They aren't evaluating a request from someone they're worried about. They're evaluating a request from someone their brain has already categorized as reliable, and those are two completely different conversations.

Small and specific isn't a coincidence here. The brain builds trust through repetition of small things, not through grand gestures. One standout demonstration of reliability carries less weight than twenty ordinary ones because the brain is building a prediction, and predictions get built from track records, not from outliers. A single remarkable performance gets filed as an outlier. Twenty ordinary follow-throughs get filed as a history. That history is what changes the prediction. It creates a new story in the mind of your parents, and that new story eventually becomes a program.

So the question isn't how to prove yourself with something big. The question is what small thing can you do today, and again tomorrow, and again the day after that, that makes your behavior more predictable than it currently is. That's where trust comes from. Every time you do it you're making a deposit into a calculation you can't see but that's absolutely running, and at some point, the calculation tips, and the rules respond.

Pick One Thing and Own It Completely

The fastest way to start building a track record is to pick one specific area, something small enough to be manageable, and own it completely for long enough that it becomes a track record the people around you can see.

This works better if the area you pick is something that matters to someone with authority in your life, because the whole point is to build a prediction in someone's brain, and the data point has to reach that brain to do any work. If you become reliable about something nobody ever notices, you get the internal benefit of having kept a commitment to yourself, which is real and worth something, but the trust math doesn't change because nobody is collecting the data. Pick something visible. Pick something that, when it consistently happens, will register with someone who currently has a low prediction of you. If they check your room regularly, a perfectly clean room is a great example because it will make them think. If it's clean consistently it will make them notice.

Six weeks is a great target. Six weeks is long enough to produce a real pattern and short enough to be concrete. Tell yourself you're going to own this one thing for six weeks, no drama, no announcement, just doing the thing. At the end of six weeks you will have a body of evidence you didn't have before, and you will know whether the thing is something you can maintain, and the people around you will have had long enough to notice a change in what they can predict about you.

The rule here is no claiming credit, *don't tell them*. The minute you tell someone what you're doing and wait to be recognized for it, you've moved the whole thing from a track record into a performance, and those are different things. A track record is what people see when they're not looking for it. A performance is what you put on when someone is watching and people know the difference, even when they can't explain how they know, and it changes how the data gets interpreted. Keep it secret, let them figure it out.

* * *

The Muscle Nobody Tells You You Have to Build

There is a word that gets used in ways that make it sound like a personality trait someone either has or doesn't have, like it's something you were born with or something that good people have and bad people lack. That word is *integrity*, and almost everything about how it gets talked about is wrong in ways that matter.

Integrity isn't a personality trait. It's a muscle, and like every muscle it exists in everyone, it's built through use, and it atrophies when it isn't used. What that means practically is that you are never reduced to being just honest or dishonest, reliable or unreliable, as a fixed category. You are currently at whatever level of development that muscle is at, based on how much you have used it, and you can increase that level starting from wherever you currently are.

Here is the precise definition, the one worth keeping: Integrity is the muscle that lets you be strong enough to do what you said you would do, when it costs you something to do it.

Read that again, because the second half is where the whole thing lives. When it *costs you* something. Keeping a commitment when it's convenient isn't a test of anything. Keeping a commitment when something came up, when you don't feel like it, when a better option appears, when nobody would know if you let it slide without a word, that's when the muscle either fires or it doesn't. That's when you either make a deposit or a withdrawal from the account that determines what you are able to do with your life. Once you're an adult, it's pretty much the only thing anyone cares about or tracks in other people.

The cost does not have to be large either, it can be small. Getting up when you said you would even though you don't want to. Following through on a commitment to a friend when something easier came along. Telling the truth in a moment when a convenient version of it would have been easier and would probably not have been checked. These small costs, paid consistently, are what build the muscle. The large tests, the ones that feel significant, are easier than they look because the muscle either already exists or it doesn't, and if it exists you just use it, and if it doesn't you can't will yourself through on the spot.

One other important thing. Integrity is mostly built in private. The moments that count most are the ones where nobody is there and the easy path is available and you do the thing anyway. That's where the muscle gets built. The public version, the part people eventually see, is just the surface of something that was built in a hundred small moments when you could have done otherwise.

You will always know when your integrity is being tested. You can feel it in the pit of your stomach because right then you know what you are supposed to do, and you also know it's going to cost you something.

* * *

The Currency That Compounds

Here is a definition of success that holds up under examination. Success is getting *access* to the things you want to do with your life. Not having the talent for them, or wanting them badly enough, and not deserving them, but getting *access*. Access, in almost every context worth talking about, is controlled by other people. People who are deciding whether to open a door, offer an opportunity, extend trust, bring you into something, invest in you.

Those people will be running the same calculation your parents are running now. They are asking whether they can predict what you will do, whether your word means something, whether the investment they make in you is going to return or disappear. Talent gets you noticed, but it's integrity that gets you chosen. The reason integrity gets you chosen, repeatedly and across contexts, is that it's rare enough that people who have resources they can allocate, always remember the people who consistently have integrity.

The word integrity shares its root with the word integer, the mathematical term for a whole number, something undivided. Structural integrity in a building means the *whole thing* holds together under load. When integrity gets applied to a person it means the same thing, it means what you do matches what you say, all the time, in every room, even when nobody is watching. An integer, all one piece, the same in every room.

This matters beyond the obvious trust-building because there's a cost to being inconsistent that people rarely name. Inconsistency requires maintaining two separate versions of yourself, the one you show people and the one you are, and managing that gap takes energy. People who have closed that gap don't spend energy on it. They aren't managing a presentation. They're just being the same person in every room, which frees up significant processing power for things that matter. This is part of why people who have built real integrity often look calmer and less reactive than people who haven't. They're not carrying the same weight.

Integrity builds its own track record, track records change predictions, positive predictions open doors, and every door you walk through gives you access to new situations where your integrity either continues to build or gets tested in ways that determine what you get access to next.

It's not something you can watch getting bigger like a bank account. It accumulates in the quality of what becomes available to you, and in the kind of person you find yourself becoming without quite being able to point to when it happened.

* * *

Start Where It Costs a Little

Don't try to start building integrity with a commitment so large that the cost of keeping it is enormous. Large commitments made before the muscle exists produce large failures, and large failures produce something the brain is going to make a protective story for, and you will get a file called "I tried that and it didn't work."

That filing is harder to undo than the original failure, so start small. Start with something where the cost of keeping the commitment is real but manageable, something that will require something from you but won't require everything.

There is a specific kind of commitment worth looking for when you're starting, which is one that nobody would notice you breaking. The dish that could have been left in the sink, that text you said you'd send, or something you said you'd look into, but nobody would check. The small follow-through that lives entirely in whether you are the kind of person who does it or doesn't, with no external enforcement, no consequence if you don't, no reward if you do except the internal one of having been the person who kept their word.

Those small, unwitnessed follow-throughs are where the muscle is built. They don't carry any heavy weight, but they are the real test. When there's no reward and no punishment and no audience and you do it anyway, that's integrity operating in its purest form. Your brain registers it. The lawyer that usually explains things away doesn't have much to work with. The data goes directly into the file of who you are, not who you are when it counts, who you are.

The progression is simple and it works, small unwitnessed commitments build the muscle, built muscle makes medium costs manageable, manageable medium costs make the larger tests something you can pass when they arrive. Nobody gets good at the large tests by attempting large tests first. They get good at them by having already kept enough small promises to themselves that the larger ones have a foundation to stand on.

Jordan was working on the same thing from a different angle. His tool was silence, and silence had built a wall that produced exactly the isolation he didn't want, and he knew it now in a way he hadn't a year before. He picked something small too, responding when people reached out, even briefly, even when it cost him something to surface from behind the wall. He didn't tell anyone he was doing it, but he kept right on doing it. The progression looked different from Marcus's because the tool was different, but the mechanism was identical. Small, unwitnessed follow-throughs, that muscle getting used and stronger, the road getting a little wider.

* * *

Marcus, October

He didn't make a big show of it. He didn't tell his stepdad what he was doing, didn't tell his mom, didn't even quite tell himself in a way he'd have been able to put into words if someone had asked.

He just started checking in before making plans. He missed some, pushed back on a few, felt the occasional flash of resentment when it seemed like more than it was worth. Still, by the third week of November his stepdad said something while passing through the kitchen. He said: "I appreciate you keeping me in the loop", and he kept walking.

Marcus didn't say anything back. He put his bowl in the sink and went to his room and stood there for a minute. The moment was small enough that nothing external had changed. No rule got dropped, nobody made a speech, the relationship was basically what it had been.

Except that one sentence had never existed before.

His stepdad had never said anything like that to him before. The reason it had never existed wasn't that his stepdad was withholding it, it was that Marcus hadn't given him any reason to say it.

That hit Marcus in a way that took a few days to settle. It wasn't a revelation, or anything big, just a tiny piece of information that kept coming back. He had been waiting for things to be different. He had been making cases for why they should be different. For the first time in a while he could see, cleanly, that *different* had required something from *him* first, that something wasn't that complicated, and that he had been the one deciding, every day, whether to do it or not.

The check-in wasn't the point, it was just one small thing he picked. The point was that he had picked it, kept it, and because he did, something had changed in stepdad's calculation, almost invisibly, because of it.

He was going to stop and start, forget, push back, resent the requirement on days when it felt like more than it was worth. That was fine, because the muscle doesn't require perfection, it requires more use than not.

He had a track record now. A small one, newer than anything, six weeks old and barely visible from the outside. But it was his, and he had built it, and nobody could take it back because nobody else had put it there.

* * *

Next: Upgrading Your Toolbox

CHAPTER SIX

Upgrading Your Toolbox

The window, the games, and why the behavior has to come before the freedom

You already know the programs weren't your fault. They were built intelligently, from real experience, for real reasons, and they were always supposed to exist. This chapter is about what comes next, and why right now is the specific time to build it.

Adolescence isn't a waiting room where you just sit around waiting for adulthood. It's a construction phase, your brain is intended to do nearly as much self-learning now, as it did when you were an infant. The myelination process that coats your neural pathways and makes signals run faster is running harder right now than it will at almost any other point in your life. Your brain is in active rebuilding mode, investing heavily in the pathways that are getting used, insulating them, strengthening them, and committing to them in ways that become increasingly difficult to change as the years go on. The mature brain rewires, but slowly and at significant cost. The adolescent brain rewires fast, by design, because this is when it's supposed to happen. Your brain is preparing for adulthood.

Neurons and Narratives

Every culture that produced functional adults understood that there is this window of time, even if nobody called it that, where you quickly learn how to be an adult. The coming-of-age tests, the apprenticeships, the rituals, the year a fourteen-year-old got handed to a craftsman in another town and came back two years later visibly different. Those weren't just traditions, they were structured interventions timed to this exact phase, because whoever designed them must have noticed that this window is when the wiring is most receptive to being rebuilt.

The programs that aren't getting replaced right now are getting reinforced. That's how myelination works. Every time the old tool fires and produces even a small amount of relief, the pathway gets a little more insulation, a little more speed, a little more automatic. The child tools don't stay neutral while you wait to address them, they get stronger. Which means the question isn't if you are gonna get an upgrade or not, the question is whether you're going to use this window because the upgrade already happened.

The potential problem with this process is that the same brain that's most receptive to building new wiring, is also most receptive to building the wrong wiring, and it will still happen fast. Myelination doesn't evaluate what it's insulating. It invests in whatever is getting used. A brain that spends *these* years practicing avoidance, or running in a group that requires certain behaviors, or numbing the discomfort instead of working through it, is myelinating those roads just as efficiently as any other. The construction phase doesn't care whether what's getting built is worth having, it just builds what gets used. That means the window is an opportunity in both directions, and knowing which direction your wiring is going right now is the most important question in this chapter. Are you building new tools that are useful for adults, or are you reinforcing childhood tools that will cause problems for you as an adult?

* * *

The Tools by Name

You know these already by now, but here they are named plainly, because having a name for something is the first step toward being able to see it.

Not My Fault. The explanation that finds some reason other than you to blame everything on, before you've finished processing what happened. Fast, automatic, relieves discomfort immediately.

Always Right. The tool that turns conceding into losing. Every disagreement becomes something that has to be won rather than something that has to be resolved.

The Exit. Leaving before things get hard. This tool gets someone to chase you after you leave. A parent coming to the door to check on you for example, or a sister who comes to see if you are ok. You get relief because someone came after you, and the relief comes from being chased, not from leaving. Trouble with this one is in adulthood, fewer and fewer people will chase you, and some that used to will now stop.

The Guilt Load. Making someone feel responsible for a consequence or a standard they're holding. It moves people who have a deep stake in your emotional state. It mostly produces discomfort and then distance in people who don't.

The Performance. The version of yourself you show people when you need something. The gap between the performance and who you really are takes longer to surface in new environments, but it does surface, and people will know the difference. You already do it, you have heard or said things like "He is always acting like" or "She is so fake".

* * *

What They Look Like After Thirty Years of Practice

In 1964, a Canadian psychiatrist named Dr. Eric Berne published a book called *Games People Play*. It spent over a hundred weeks on the New York Times bestseller list, sold more than five million copies, and is still in print today. Berne's central finding was that most of the painful, repetitive, unproductive interactions people have with each other follow scripts. Predictable sequences with predictable outcomes, running without conscious awareness, producing the same results over and over across decades.

Berne called these scripts games, a name that has nothing to do with fun. A game, in his framework, is a series of transactions that follows a structured sequence toward some "payoff" that a person is unconsciously steering toward, usually one that *confirms an existing story* about themselves or the world. The people are almost never aware they're doing it. They just find themselves in the same situation again, with the same result, and a perfectly reasonable explanation for why.

He identified dozens of them. Here are five you've probably already seen play out, at home, at school, in the adults around you, and if you're paying close attention, in yourself.

You know someone who always has a problem. You offer a solution. They explain why that won't work. You try another one, and that also won't work. You keep going until you give up and not once was anything you had to offer good enough. Here's the thing… They weren't looking for a solution, they were looking for confirmation that nothing can be done, because if nothing can be done, they don't have to do anything. Berne called this one *Why Don't You / Yes But*, and once you see it you can't unsee it.

Something goes wrong for someone and it immediately becomes your fault. Not in an obvious way, more like, they were about to do it right and then you distracted them, or they would have handled it if you hadn't put them in that position. The mistake is always real, but it's always your fault they did it. The payoff is that they never have to look at their own behavior, because there's always a reason it wasn't them. In every team, every partnership, every household where this runs, accountability becomes impossible. Berne called this one *See What You Made Me Do.*

There's always a reason, and the reason always has a name. The job they couldn't take, the thing they couldn't try, the version of themselves they could have been, all of it blocked by the same person, the same situation, the same circumstance that keeps showing up as the explanation. The payoff is something to blame for every limitation, which means they never have to look at what they're contributing. Some people spend decades narrating their lives as a series of things that were done to them. Berne called this one *If It Weren't For You.*

Two people who get together and love to complain about how bad everything is. The school, the parents, the situation, the people who don't get it. It feels like connection, and in a way it is, but it's a connection built entirely on complaint, and it requires both people to keep finding things to be angry about to keep the bond alive. Nobody gets better at anything. Nobody solves anything. The relationship runs on shared misery and calls itself friendship. Berne called this one *Ain't It Awful.*

Someone has a reason why the rules don't apply to them. Maybe it's something that happened to them, maybe it's something about how they are, maybe it's just a hard situation they're in. And it's always available. Every time there's an expectation, the reason shows up. Every time something doesn't get done, the reason explains it. The limitation might even be real. Berne's point wasn't that the hardship is fake, his point was that the hardship became a permanent excuse for never building what they were capable of. He called it *Wooden Leg*.

Remember, Berne was describing adults. People in marriages, in workplaces, in therapy offices, the very people who want everyone to believe they have everything worked out. He wasn't writing about teenagers, he was documenting what the *child-level tools* look like when they've had thirty or forty years of myelination behind them and nobody ever built anything to replace them. These aren't personality types, they're what happens when the software doesn't get upgraded along with the hardware. When the window closes and the old programs are still the only programs running.

You've seen adults doing all of this, running these programs, playing these games. You probably recognized them before you had names for them. Now you have names for them, and you have something those adults mostly don't have. For you, the window is still open.

There's one more environment worth naming here, because it's one where these programs run harder and faster than almost anywhere else: the internet. Social media in particular is a purpose-built arena for the child tools. *Why Don't You / Yes But* thrives in comment sections. *Ain't It Awful* is the operating model of entire platforms. *The Performance* gets a professional-grade stage with audience metrics attached. The tools that cost you in person cost you more online because the feedback loop is faster, the audience is larger, and the distance makes the consequences easier to ignore until they're not. This isn't an argument against being online. It's a reason to know what you're running when you get there, because the window applies to what you're practicing online just as much as what you're practicing in the room.

* * *

Why the Freedom Isn't Arriving

In their mind, your parents are running an outdated version of you. The programs they use to interact with you were written when you were younger, in a relationship where the dynamic was clear and the roles were fixed, and those programs update slowly, the same way all programs update, which is through consistent new evidence repeated over time.

The problem is that most of the evidence coming in has been in the child tools. Arguing for freedom that hasn't been demonstrated yet, *exiting* when the conversation gets hard, *loading the guilt* when a boundary holds or running *the performance* when something is needed. All of that goes through your parents' programs and comes back with the same label it always has, "This is someone who still needs to be managed, not someone ready for more."

It's worth being clear about the word "childish" because it tends to feel like an insult when it's a description. Childish means the behavior belongs to childhood. That's where it was built, that's where it worked, and that's what it's called. You would never say "stop being childish" to a four year old. They're FOUR, they are *supposed* to be childish.

So it's more like a location than it is a verdict. The behavior was right for that stage, it was fine then. Running it past that stage is what makes it childish, not the person running it.

Every culture that produced functional adults had a version of the same basic transaction. Here's the test. Pass it and you cross over. The specifics varied everywhere, but the structure was identical, demonstrate the behaviors this community requires of adults, and we'll treat you as one. The test existed because the community understood something we kind of ignore now, we certainly don't talk about it plainly. Freedom and responsibility aren't separate things that arrive at different times, they're the *same transaction*. You don't get one without evidence of the other.

The formal test may be gone, but the transaction didn't go anywhere. It's happening right now, in your house, at your school, and eventually in every workplace and relationship you'll ever enter. The adults in your life are running the same calculation they will always run, "Is this person showing me the behaviors that make it safe to extend more trust?"

The test is informal, unannounced, and ongoing. You're already in it, and YOU are going to run exactly the same test on the people around you, for the rest of your life.

So here's the piece that changes everything, if you want adult freedom, you have to *behave* yourself into it. The behavior comes first, the freedom follows. Adults aren't just keeping you from freedom on a whim or because it's fun. That's just how this transaction has always worked, in every culture, in every era, and it's going to keep working that way in every adult environment you ever find yourself in.

This isn't just about your parents, it's about every relationship. Every job, every partnership, every situation across your entire adult life that requires other people to decide whether to trust you with something. The parent relationship is the first arena, this is where you are usually supposed to practice. The tools you build now, while the window is open and the myelination is running, are the ones you carry into all of it.

Look if home isn't a safe or functional place to practice any of this, the arena doesn't have to be home. The transaction between behavior and trust runs everywhere. A teacher who's noticed you showing up differently, a friend group where your track record is still being written, a job, a coach, a mentor. Any environment where someone is watching and the data is still fresh. The work doesn't require a cooperative home environment to start. It requires one relationship where the evidence can land. Start wherever it works and feels safe for you, but *start*.

*　*　*

What Gets Built Instead

The adult tools aren't about being a different person. They're about having tools that work in environments that don't know your history and have no particular obligation to absorb what your family absorbed.

Ownership without collapse is the replacement for Not My Fault. It requires separating the two things that a child tool fused together. Being responsible for an outcome, and being a bad person because of it. From now on when you do something that produces a result, you own it, you figure out what to do differently, and who you are doesn't become the mistake. Your lawyer spent years building the case that owning things was dangerous. Building this tool means running a different program in the same situations, enough times that the new road starts getting some myelin on it.

Conceding when you're wrong is the replacement for Always Right. This isn't giving in to avoid conflict, which is another tool developed in childhood. Instead it's recognizing when the other person's opinion or solution is better than yours and saying so clearly. It tells people you're more interested in getting it right than n *being* right, and that information compounds over time. People who can concede clearly are rare and they get trusted with more.

Following through without being reminded. Less a specific behavior than a standard. The child tool was to follow through when someone was checking. The adult tool is to follow through because you said you would, with no checking required. The environments you're moving into don't have bandwidth to track your commitments for you. This one gets built exactly where the last chapter described, in the small unwitnessed moments where you do the thing with no audience and no enforcement.

The honest no. Most people think the adult move is to say yes more. The adult move is to say no when you can't do the thing well, or don't have time to do it right, or know that saying yes is going to produce a miss. An honest no given upfront is worth way more than a yes followed by a failure to deliver, because a yes followed by a miss trains the people around you to verify your commitments, and that's a reputation that's slow to fix.

Staying to repair is the replacement for the exit. It requires staying in a hard conversation past the point of comfort. Repair doesn't mean agreement by the way, it means acknowledging that a rupture happened and taking some ownership of getting back to solid ground. The people who can do this are the ones others build real things with, because real things require dealing with real friction, and friction requires someone who stays.

* * *

What the Transition Looks Like

Here's something worth knowing before you try any of this. For a while, both sets of tools are live at the same time.

The old programs don't go offline the moment you decide to build something new. They're faster, more practiced, more deeply myelinated, and they fire in situations that feel familiar before you've had time to choose anything. You're going to be in a hard conversation and intend to stay, but then the exit happens before you've finished deciding not to take it. You're going to mean to own something, when the excuse will pop into your head and be out of your mouth before you knew it was loading. That's not failure! This is what building looks like when the new road is still thin and the old road is wide and fast.

The mistake many people make at this point is treating the misfire as evidence that nothing has changed, that the new tool doesn't work, or that they're just someone who runs the old program and that's that. The misfire isn't evidence of any of those things. It only proves that the old pathway has more myelin than the new one, which is exactly what you'd expect at this stage, and the only thing that changes the ratio is use. Every time you catch the old tool loading, even after it's fired, and do something different in the recovery, the new road gets a little more investment. The old programs don't get weaker by being condemned. They get weaker by being used less and replaced by something that gets used more.

The recovery matters as much as the catch. If the exit happens and you come back to repair the conversation, that's the new tool running. It ran late, after the old one fired first, *but it ran.* The brain doesn't need you to stop the old program in the moment. It just needs you to run the new one enough times, and in the same territory so that it starts competing for the road.

The other thing worth knowing is that the people around you are going to be slow to update, your parents especially. The programs they're running have you filed under a specific label, and a few instances of new behavior aren't going to immediately rewrite what years of evidence built. They'll notice inconsistency before they notice change. They will wonder if it's the performance. They may not say anything at all for weeks. This isn't them being unfair. It's just their programs running the same process that all programs run, which is slow, evidence-based, and resistant to revision until the new pattern is too consistent to explain away. You're producing data. The update comes when the data stacks. *Keep Going.*

It's worth knowing because a lot of people try the new tools for a few weeks, see that the environment hasn't responded the way they hoped, figure it isn't working, and then go back to what's familiar. The environment lagging is never proof the tools aren't working. It's a normal delay between behavior change and prediction change, and it's the same delay that Chapter Five described in the context of building a track record. You're building one now, across a larger set of behaviors. The math is the same, only the timeline is longer.

* * *

What It Looks Like When It Runs

The adult tools don't each produce a separate result in a separate category of your life, they stack up on top of one another. Each one builds the same underlying thing, a track record of being someone whose behavior is predictable in the specific ways that make people willing to invest in you.

Ownership without collapse tells people you can be handed responsibility and it won't disappear into an excuse when something goes wrong. Conceding tells people the way you see things can be trusted because you'll change your mind when the evidence changes. Following through without being reminded tells people what you say and what you do are the same thing. The honest no tells people a yes from you *means something* because you don't hand them out to manage the moment. Staying to repair tells people that when things get hard, you're still going to be there.

Each of those is a separate data point, but together they build a single thing in the brain of everyone who's watching, "This is someone I can rely on."

That reputation doesn't arrive on a birthday. It builds the way all track records build: slowly, through repetition of small things, in ordinary situations, over time. It builds in the same direction across every environment you enter, because the tools that earn it are the same tools in every room.

The child tools were calibrated for one specific environment and stopped working when the environment changed. The adult tools are calibrated for adult life, which means they work in the classroom, the friend group, the first job, the long-term relationship, and every environment after that. You're not building something that works here and stops working later. You're building something that travels.

That's what the window is for. That's what the myelination is investing in. Not just getting your parents to ease up, and just surviving the teen years with fewer arguments. It is building the wiring that makes the rest of your life work the way you want it to.

* * *

Marcus, November

The friend group had a project due Friday. Marcus had been in the group two weeks, new enough that nobody had a fixed read on him yet, which was the kind of opening he usually moved through well.

Wednesday night Darius texted asking about the slides. Marcus said he'd handle them. He'd meant to start, hadn't, and now it was nine and Darius was asking where they were.

The tool loaded fast, Darius hadn't confirmed a timeline, nobody had checked in earlier if it mattered that much. The excuse was forming, finding its shape, getting solid.

He paused.

He hadn't decided anything really, it was more like something snagged. The moment in the kitchen three weeks ago was still somewhere at the back of his head, not the sentence his stepdad had said but what came after it, what had taken a few days to settle. He was now looking at the same mechanism in a different room. Same tool, different people, people who had no history with him and no particular reason to absorb what his family had absorbed.

He typed: "Sorry, got behind. Working on them now, can have them done by midnight."

Then he opened the slides and started.

They were done at 11:40. Darius said thanks, the project was fine. Nothing external changed.

His stepdad wasn't going to suddenly trust him more because of a Wednesday night nobody else knew about. Darius didn't know what it had cost Marcus to type that message instead of the other one. The people in Marcus's life were still running whatever version of him they'd built over years of evidence, and one night wasn't touching that.

But Marcus knew that, he wasn't expecting anything different.

What had happened was small and specific, a tool had loaded, he'd caught it loading, and he'd run something different. The tool was still wired in, still going to load in the next situation before he had time to think. He knew that too.

But the new road had gotten a little use. A small deposit into a track record that didn't exist yet. One data point in a direction nobody had enough of yet to call a pattern.

He understood, in a way he couldn't quite put into words, that this was how it worked. Not in moments anyone was watching or in gestures that announced themselves. On a Wednesday night when nobody knew, and the slides got done, and the new road got just a little wider than it had been before.

* * *

Next: The New Normal

CHAPTER SEVEN

The New Normal

What changes, what doesn't, and what you're carrying forward

Marcus's stepdad didn't sit him down and give a speech.

There was no single moment where someone acknowledged the work he'd been doing or told him they'd noticed a change. His mom didn't pull him aside. His stepdad didn't bring up the kitchen conversation from October or the slides from November or the dozen small things in between. Nobody said anything. The world didn't rearrange itself into a different shape and then pause to let him appreciate the view.

What happened instead was smaller and more specific and, once Marcus understood what he was looking at, more meaningful than a speech would have been.

In January his stepdad asked him to pick up his younger stepsister from soccer practice on a Thursday. Not with a backup plan built in, not with a reminder text at 3:45, not with a "just make sure you do it this time" attached to the ask. It was just: "Can you get her Thursday?", and then he moved on to something else, as if the answer was assumed.

Marcus picked her up. He didn't think much about it until later that night when he realized what had been different about how the ask landed. His stepdad hadn't checked. There had been no verification mechanism built into the request. The ask had been made the way you make an ask to someone whose answer you don't need to verify.

Nobody told him that his stepdad's prediction of him had changed. Nobody held a ceremony celebrating this change in the program. The rules had been loosening in ways Marcus noticed but hadn't connected, and it was only now that he connected them. Marcus changed the way he did a few things, that data had stacked up. The next time stepdad ran the calculation, the prediction was updated. This thing he'd been building since October, one small unwitnessed deposit at a time, had built something.

This is how the new normal arrives. Without any warning or acknowledgement. Someone just asks for something without a backup plan, or just starts saying thank you for little things, or treats you a little more like an adult without even knowing they did it.

* * *

How the People Around You Update

The environment doesn't update the way you might hope it does, which is immediately and with acknowledgment. It updates the way all systems do, slowly, based on evidence, and usually after you've started to wonder if anything is changing at all.

This is the part that breaks a lot of people's momentum. They do the work for a few weeks, they notice the environment hasn't visibly changed, and they decide either that the work isn't enough or that the people around them are never going to change. Both of those conclusions can feel completely accurate and still be wrong, because the update is happening in a place you can't see. It's in the recalculation running underneath the surface of every interaction, in the slow revision of a prediction that was built over years and requires consistent new evidence to move.

Your parents' programs have you filed under that label we talked about. A label that was built from real observations over a long time. A few weeks of different behavior isn't going to erase it. What it does is start introducing data that doesn't fit the existing file. At first, their program explains it away "This is the performance, this is temporary", and they wait for it to go back to the way it was. But when the evidence keeps arriving, then the file starts getting complicated. Finally at some point that's impossible to predict and won't be announced, the label gets revised. *Their program gets updated.*

That revision shows up in little ways first. The way an ask gets phrased or if a request comes with a backup plan built in. Whether the default assumption in a conversation is that you're going to be a problem or that you're going to be fine. These aren't things most people pay attention to, but they register in the brain, and over time the accumulation of them is what the new normal feels like from the inside.

The update also moves outward. The parent relationship is the first arena where you're building the new track record, but it's not the only place the data goes. Teachers, coaches, friends, anyone who's been operating on an old prediction of you is running the same update process at their own pace. You're producing data. The data reaches different people at different times. The environment changes around you in layers, and the layers know about each other. Each builds in its own time, each changes when it's ready, so be patient and keep going.

* * *

What the New Normal Doesn't Mean

Problems won't stop, adults still have problems. This is worth saying clearly because there could be another version of this chapter that would read like a promise that if you do the work, life gets easier, but that version would be dishonest.

Hard things will keep happening, people will still be unfair sometimes. Situations will still go wrong. You will still end up in conversations that are difficult, relationships that require more than you expected, and environments where the rules seem stacked in a direction that isn't yours. The new normal doesn't change any of that. What it changes is what you're meeting those things with.

The old tools met hard things by finding someone to blame, finding an excuse, exiting, loading the performance, or building a case. Those responses reduced the discomfort of the moment, provided relief, while accumulating cost in the background. The new tools meet hard things by staying present, taking ownership of the part that's yours, saying no when a yes would set you up to fail, and repairing when something breaks. Those responses cost more in the moment and accumulate something different in the background.

What accumulates is capacity. The more you use the new tools in hard situations, the more myelinated those pathways get, the faster they fire, the more automatic they become, until staying to repair doesn't require the same effort it required the first time you did it. Owning an outcome doesn't produce the same collapse it used to, and the honest no comes out with less friction than it once cost. The hard things don't get smaller. Your capacity for them grows.

The other thing the new normal doesn't mean is that the old tools disappear. They don't, you know this. They're wired in, they're faster than the new ones will be for a long time, and they're going to fire in situations that feel familiar before you've had a chance to choose. The new normal isn't the permanent absence of the old programs. It's a gradually changing ratio where the old programs fire less often, catch themselves faster, get recovered from more quickly, and produce a smaller version of the old result. The gap between loading and firing that Marcus found on a Thursday in October and a Wednesday in November gets wider. That gap is where the new behavior lives.

* * *

What You're Carrying Forward

Every environment you enter from here is one where the adult tools work and the child tools cost.

The classroom where you're trying to build a relationship with a teacher who doesn't know you yet. The friend group where nobody has a read on you and the first few months of data are going to determine what slot they put you in. The job you're going to want eventually, where someone is going to make a decision about whether you're worth investing in based on a track record you're building from the first week. The partnership, the collaboration, the situation where someone has to decide whether to trust you with something that matters to them.

In all of those environments, the calculation is the same one your parents are running.

Can I predict what this person will do? Does what they say match what they do? When something goes wrong, do they own it or do they find the excuse? When things get hard, do they stay or do they exit?

The people running those calculations aren't your parents and don't have your history. They're building their prediction of you from scratch, from the data you give them starting from the first interaction.

The child tools would produce the same result they always have, a prediction that closes doors. The adult tools produce a different result, a prediction that opens those same doors. The reason this matters so much right now, in this specific phase, is that the wiring you're building during the myelination window is the wiring you're going to bring with you into those environments. You're not starting over in each new place. You're bringing what you built here.

This is what the window is for. Not just getting your parents to ease up or just surviving the teen years with fewer arguments. Building the specific wiring that makes the rest of your life work the way you want it to, in every room you walk into for the next several decades, with people who have no obligation to absorb what your family absorbed and every reason to take you at face value based on the evidence you give them.

The teen years aren't a rehearsal for real life. They *are* real life, and the construction is real, what gets built is real, and it travels.

* * *

What to Do With What You Know Now

What you have now isn't a test to pass or a standard to meet. It's a set of names for programs that were already running, and names help because you can't work with something you can't see. You can see the lawyer now, you can see the programs, and you can see the gap between the tool loading and the tool firing. You know what the window is and why it's there. You know why the test exists even when nobody names it and that you're already in it. There are no rules now for what you do with all this. It's all yours to use or not, in your own time, in the situations where you decide to use it. Seeing is the first move, everything else is just the next one.

There's no threshold where the work is finished, no point where the wiring is complete and you can stop paying attention. The adult brain keeps building and pruning for a long time, and the tools require use to stay sharp. The track record keeps being built from whatever data you're currently producing, and the work you start now isn't work you do once and finish. It's a practice, and the practice is what the rest of your life runs on.

Start where it costs a little. Pick one tool to work on. Run it in a single situation first. Don't tell anyone about it or wait for recognition. Let the track record build from the inside out, in those tiny unwitnessed moments where the only one who knows is you.

Knowing is enough, because the brain is recording it regardless of whether anyone else is watching.

* * *

Marcus, February

He was sitting in the car waiting for his stepsister when he thought about Chapter One.

Not the chapter in this book, but the chapter of his own story, the one that had been running since before he had words for it. The stepjerk who was unreasonable. That teacher who had it out for him. His father who kept canceling. The complete and total explanation for why his life was the way it was, and the explanation never once including Marcus.

He wasn't that person anymore. He wasn't sure exactly when it had started to change, because it hadn't started with a decision. It had started with a lag on a Thursday in October when the program loaded slower than usual, and a text he sent in November instead of the one he'd meant to send, and a check-in he kept doing without announcing it, and a slide deck that got done at 11:40 on a Wednesday night when nobody was watching.

His dad still canceled sometimes, that hadn't changed and probably wasn't going to. Marcus had spent a long time filing that as "things outside of me cause pain, and there's not much I can do about it" and he still felt it. The program still loaded when a plan fell through. What was different was that he didn't need that filing to mean something about him anymore. His dad's choices were his dad's choices. The pain was real and he had to deal with that, but it didn't have to be his explanation for everything else.

His stepdad still issued rules and some of them still felt unnecessary. Marcus pushed back on some, more calmly than he used to, and sometimes his stepdad explained the reason and sometimes he didn't, and either way Marcus did the thing more often than he didn't, and the doing was building into something he could feel even when he couldn't measure it. His mom still had the "tone" sometimes, of course moms always will. But Ms. Patterson had started staying after class to talk about his essays, which was something that hadn't happened in ninth grade.

His lawyer was still there, and it still loaded fast. It still handed him a story in the first half-second after something went wrong, a built in excuse with a case fully formed. The exit was available and the performance was ready if he needed them. His programs didn't go away after all, they just had some competition now, and the competition was getting faster.

His stepsister knocked on the car window and he unlocked the door and she got in and immediately started talking about something that happened at practice, some drama he was going to have to listen to for the whole drive home. He listened, he asked questions. He kept his eyes on the road.

He was fifteen. He had most of his life still ahead of him, and all of it was going to require other people to decide to trust him or not, and the wiring he was building right now was the wiring he was going to take with him everywhere.

That wasn't a burden, it was just the situation. The situation was his, and he was the one deciding what to do with it, one Thursday afternoon at a time.

* * *

A Note Before You Go

The parents reading their own version of this book are getting the same information from the other side. They're reading about the upgrade, about the programs their own brains built, about how the version of you they've been running needs new data to update. They're being asked to do the same work you're being asked to do, which is to see the program as a program and decide to run something different.

This goes both directions. It always has. The friction between teenagers and the adults in their lives isn't a character problem on either side. It's two sets of programs, built for different situations, running into each other in the same household, in a phase where both sides are being asked to update simultaneously without a manual.

The update is possible, the work is real, and the window is open.

Start now.

Appendix D
The Science Behind This Book
Source notes and research for each major topic

This book explains real neuroscience in plain language. Every major claim about how the brain works, how adolescent development unfolds, and how behavior becomes automatic is grounded in peer-reviewed research. This appendix organizes the underlying science by topic, explains what the research shows, and provides full citations so you can go deeper on anything that interests you.

The citations follow APA 7th edition format. Where research is ongoing or findings are nuanced, those nuances are noted.

1. Myelination: How Behavior Becomes Automatic

The book describes myelin as insulation that wraps neural pathways and makes signals travel faster — transforming deliberate, effortful responses into fast, automatic ones. This is an accurate lay summary of a well-established neurobiological process.

What the research shows

Myelin is a fatty substance produced by oligodendrocyte cells that wraps around axons (the signal-carrying extensions of neurons). Myelinated axons conduct electrical signals up to 100 times faster than unmyelinated ones. Once a pathway is myelinated, the behavior it supports becomes faster, more automatic, and increasingly difficult to override deliberately. This is why practiced behaviors — from riding a bike to emotional responses to social situations — become reflexive over time.

Critically, myelination is not neutral. Pathways that are used frequently get myelinated; pathways that go unused are pruned (see Section 3 on synaptic pruning). The brain invests in what gets practiced. Avoidance, deflection, and withdrawal myelinate just as efficiently as engagement, accountability, and repair. The behavioral implications of this are central to the book's argument.

Blakemore and Choudhury (2006) provide the most widely cited review of myelination during adolescence. They note that while sensory and motor regions are fully myelinated in the first few years of life, frontal cortex axons — those supporting executive function, judgment, and impulse control — continue myelinating through adolescence and into early adulthood. This means the brain regions most relevant to decision-making are among the last to achieve full conduction efficiency.

Primary sources

Blakemore, S. J., & Choudhury, S. (2006). Development of the adolescent brain: Implications for executive function and social cognition. Journal of Child Psychology and Psychiatry, 47(3–4), 296–312. https://doi.org/10.1111/j.1469-7610.2006.01611.x

Giedd, J. N., Blumenthal, J., Jeffries, N. O., Castellanos, F. X., Liu, H., Zijdenbos, A., Rapoport, J. L. (1999). Brain development during childhood and adolescence: A longitudinal MRI study. Nature Neuroscience, 2(10), 861–863. https://doi.org/10.1038/13158

Gogtay, N., Giedd, J. N., Lusk, L., Hayashi, K. M., Greenstein, D., Vaituzis, A. C., Thompson, P. M. (2004). Dynamic mapping of human cortical development during childhood through early adulthood. Proceedings of the National Academy of Sciences, 101(21), 8174–8179. https://doi.org/10.1073/pnas.0402680101

2. Adolescent Brain Development: The Upgrade

The book describes adolescence as a period of significant neurological restructuring, in which the limbic system (handling emotion, status, and social connection) gains power and sensitivity while the prefrontal cortex (handling judgment, impulse control, and consequences) lags significantly behind — not reaching full maturity until the mid-twenties. This is among the most consistently replicated findings in developmental neuroscience.

The limbic–prefrontal imbalance

Structural MRI studies conducted at the National Institute of Mental Health by Jay Giedd and colleagues across the 1990s and 2000s provided the first large-scale longitudinal evidence of this developmental gap. Their work showed that subcortical limbic regions involved in emotional reactivity mature earlier, while the prefrontal cortex — responsible for regulation, planning, and evaluating consequences — is among the very last brain structures to fully mature, continuing development through the mid-twenties.

Casey and colleagues (2008) built on this work to propose the "dual systems" model of adolescent behavior: heightened responsiveness to incentives and socioemotional cues (driven by maturing limbic systems) combined with immature prefrontal regulatory control produces the characteristic pattern of adolescent risk-taking and emotional reactivity. This is not a character flaw. It is the expected output of a brain in which the accelerator is running ahead of the brakes.

The prefrontal cortex controls exactly the capacities the book discusses: consequences, long-term thinking, impulse control, weighing decisions, and owning outcomes. The consistent research finding that this region does not reach full maturity until approximately age 25 is the neurobiological basis for the book's entire argument about the adolescent window.

Gender differences in timing

The book notes that the limbic upgrade tends to arrive earlier in girls (often beginning around age 10 or 11) and that boys tend to show a wider and longer gap between emotional power and regulatory capacity. These timing differences are documented in Giedd et al. (1999) and replicated across multiple subsequent studies. The practical implication — that girls may experience the emotional intensity earlier and boys may face the regulatory gap for longer — is consistent across the literature, though individual variation is substantial.

Status as a survival signal

The book describes the upgraded adolescent brain treating status and identity as urgent in the same way it treats physical survival — noting that this is why correction can feel like a threat, and why being wrong in front of peers can feel physically painful. This is supported by neuroimaging research showing heightened amygdala and striatal reactivity to social evaluation during adolescence compared to childhood or adulthood. The adolescent brain processes social threat and physical threat through overlapping neural circuitry.

Primary sources

Casey, B. J., Getz, S., & Galvan, A. (2008). The adolescent brain. Annals of the New York Academy of Sciences, 1124, 111–126. https://doi.org/10.1196/annals.1440.010

Giedd, J. N., Blumenthal, J., Jeffries, N. O., Castellanos, F. X., Liu, H., Zijdenbos, A., Rapoport, J. L. (1999). Brain development during childhood and adolescence: A longitudinal MRI study. Nature Neuroscience, 2(10), 861–863. https://doi.org/10.1038/13158

Arain, M., Haque, M., Johal, L., Mathur, P., Nel, W., Rais, A., Sharma, S. (2013). Maturation of the adolescent brain. Neuropsychiatric Disease and Treatment, 9, 449–461. https://doi.org/10.2147/NDT.S39776

Steinberg, L. (2008). A social neuroscience perspective on adolescent risk-taking. Developmental Review, 28(1), 78–106. https://doi.org/10.1016/j.dr.2007.08.002

3. Synaptic Pruning: The Brain Deciding What to Keep

The book describes synaptic pruning as the process by which the brain cuts connections that go unused and strengthens ones that get used, building the neural architecture of adulthood around the habits already in place during adolescence. This is accurate and well-documented.

What the research shows

The human brain builds an enormous overabundance of neural connections in early childhood — far more than will be kept. Adolescence is when the brain begins large-scale pruning: eliminating connections that have not been regularly used and reinforcing the ones that have. The result is a brain that is leaner, faster, and more efficient — but also more committed to the pathways it has kept.

Giedd and colleagues documented this process through longitudinal MRI studies showing that gray matter volume peaks in early adolescence and then declines — reflecting the pruning of synaptic connections — while white matter (myelinated axonal pathways) continues to increase. The brain is simultaneously cutting the old and investing in the used.

The behavioral implication is exactly what the book describes: the adolescent brain is literally building the neural architecture it will carry into adulthood, and it is doing so based on what has been getting practiced. The timing of this process — running at maximum during adolescence when judgment is still developing and the emotional system is loudest — is the specific combination the book is written around.

Primary sources

Giedd, J. N. (2004). Structural magnetic resonance imaging of the adolescent brain. Annals of the New York Academy of Sciences, 1021, 77–85. https://doi.org/10.1196/annals.1308.009

Huttenlocher, P. R. (1979). Synaptic density in human frontal cortex: Developmental changes and effects of aging. Brain Research, 163(2), 195–205. https://doi.org/10.1016/0006-8993(79)90349-4

Blakemore, S. J., & Choudhury, S. (2006). Development of the adolescent brain: Implications for executive function and social cognition. Journal of Child Psychology and Psychiatry, 47(3–4), 296–312. https://doi.org/10.1111/j.1469-7610.2006.01611.x

4. Prefrontal Cortex Maturity: The Mid-Twenties Finding

The book states that the prefrontal cortex does not finish developing until the mid-twenties. This is one of the most consistently replicated and widely cited findings in developmental neuroscience, supported by structural MRI, diffusion tensor imaging, and behavioral studies across multiple research groups.

What the research shows

The prefrontal cortex (PFC) is the brain's center for executive function: consequences, long-term planning, impulse control, decision-making, and evaluating the impact of behavior on others. Multiple lines of evidence converge on the finding that full PFC maturation is not achieved until approximately age 25. These include structural MRI studies showing continued gray matter changes and white matter growth through early adulthood, diffusion tensor imaging showing continued myelination of frontal white matter tracts, and behavioral studies showing that impulse control and risk-calibrated decision-making continue improving through the mid-twenties.

Casey's testimony to the U.S. Sentencing Commission (2024) summarizes the convergent evidence: impulsive, short-sighted decision-making continues to decline throughout the twenties, and the development of prefrontal cortex connections with other brain networks facilitates improved executive functioning well into young adulthood. This body of evidence is the basis for the book's use of the mid-twenties as the developmental endpoint.

Primary sources

Arain, M., Haque, M., Johal, L., Mathur, P., Nel, W., Rais, A., Sharma, S. (2013). Maturation of the adolescent brain. Neuropsychiatric Disease and Treatment, 9, 449–461. https://doi.org/10.2147/NDT.S39776

Casey, B. J. (2024). Written testimony of B.J. Casey, Ph.D. [Submitted to the United States Sentencing Commission].

https://www.ussc.gov/sites/default/files/pdf/amendment-process/public-hearings-and-meetings/20240306-07/casey.pdf

Steinberg, L., Graham, S., O'Brien, L., Woolard, J., Cauffman, E., & Banich, M. (2009). Age differences in future orientation and delay discounting. Child Development, 80(1), 28–44. https://doi.org/10.1111/j.1467-8624.2008.01244.x

5. The Amygdala, Hypothalamus, and the Threat Response

The book describes the amygdala as the brain structure that compares new situations against stored patterns and flags familiar ones as confirmed, and the hypothalamus as the command center that normalizes the body's stress response when the amygdala signals that a situation is already explained. This is an accurate functional description of these structures and their role in maintaining existing belief patterns.

What the research shows

The amygdala plays a central role in evaluating incoming information for threat or reward, and in triggering emotional responses. Critically for the book's argument, the amygdala operates through pattern-matching against prior experience — it evaluates new situations based on what it already knows. When a new experience matches an existing explanation, the amygdala signals familiarity, which activates the hypothalamus's homeostatic function: restoring calm, reducing cortisol, and allowing the nervous system to return to baseline.

The practical effect described in the book — that the body's return to normal feels like confirmation that the story is true — is consistent with research on the relationship between somatic states and belief formation. The body's sense of relief and normalcy provides a signal that the brain interprets as correctness, even when the explanation is inaccurate or self-serving. This is part of why changing a well-established narrative is physiologically uncomfortable: new information that challenges an existing story activates the stress response rather than resolving it.

Research on the adolescent amygdala shows heightened sensitivity and reactivity compared to adults — the system is louder and faster during these years, which amplifies the confirmation-of-story effect the book describes.

Primary sources

Casey, B. J., Getz, S., & Galvan, A. (2008). The adolescent brain. Annals of the New York Academy of Sciences, 1124, 111–126. https://doi.org/10.1196/annals.1440.010

LeDoux, J. E. (2000). Emotion circuits in the brain. Annual Review of Neuroscience, 23, 155–184. https://doi.org/10.1146/annurev.neuro.23.1.155

Tottenham, N., & Galván, A. (2016). Stress and the adolescent brain: Amygdala-prefrontal cortex circuitry and ventral striatum as developmental targets. Neuroscience & Biobehavioral Reviews, 70, 217–227. https://doi.org/10.1016/j.neubiorev.2016.07.030

6. Social Belonging and the Adolescent Brain

The book describes the need for social belonging as a biological drive during adolescence — one that the upgraded brain treats with the same urgency as physical safety, because for most of human history social belonging and physical survival were the same thing. It then draws the connection between this drive and the risk of friend group and gang involvement during the myelination window. Both claims are supported by research.

Belonging as a survival-level signal

Neuroscience research confirms that social exclusion and social belonging activate overlapping neural circuitry with physical threat and physical safety. During adolescence, the brain's sensitivity to social evaluation and social belonging is particularly heightened. Imaging studies show that the prospect of social exclusion activates the same threat-detection systems as physical danger, and that social acceptance activates reward pathways in ways that are especially intense during adolescent development.

Peer influence and behavior during adolescence

Steinberg and colleagues have produced extensive research showing that adolescents are disproportionately influenced by peers in ways that adults are not, and that risk-taking behavior in adolescents is specifically amplified by peer presence in ways that have clear neural correlates. The presence of peers activates the brain's reward circuitry in adolescents to a degree not seen in adults, which helps explain why group membership and social belonging have particularly strong behavioral effects during these years.

The behavioral implication for gang involvement and friend selection follows directly: if the myelination window is open, and the brain is building its architecture around whatever the group practices, the specific behaviors the group requires will be among the most heavily reinforced patterns during the most plastic period of development. This is not a character claim. It is a straightforward application of myelination research to peer-group dynamics.

Primary sources

Gardner, M., & Steinberg, L. (2005). Peer influence on risk taking, risk preference, and risky decision making in adolescence and adulthood: An experimental study. Developmental Psychology, 41(4), 625–635. https://doi.org/10.1037/0012-1649.41.4.625

Eisenberger, N. I., Lieberman, M. D., & Williams, K. D. (2003). Does rejection hurt? An fMRI study of social exclusion. Science, 302(5643), 290–292. https://doi.org/10.1126/science.1089134

Galvan, A., Hare, T. A., Parra, C. E., Penn, J., Voss, H., Glover, G., & Casey, B. J. (2006). Earlier development of the accumbens relative to orbitofrontal cortex might underlie risk-taking behavior in adolescents. Journal of Neuroscience, 26(25), 6885–6892. https://doi.org/10.1523/JNEUROSCI.1973-06.2006

7. Cannabis and the Developing Brain

The book states that THC, the active compound in cannabis, directly disrupts prefrontal cortex development during adolescence; that this disruption is specific to the developmental window and not equivalent to adult cannabis use; and that research consistently associates adolescent cannabis use with measurable lasting reductions in the functions the teen brain most needs to develop. This is an accurate summary of the current research consensus, with important nuances noted below.

THC and prefrontal development

Cannabinoid CB1 receptors are densely concentrated in the hippocampus, prefrontal cortex, and amygdala — precisely the regions undergoing the most active development during adolescence. THC binds to these receptors and interferes with the normal developmental processes occurring in those regions. Preclinical animal studies show that adolescent THC exposure disrupts synaptic pruning, alters GABAergic inhibition in the prefrontal cortex, and produces lasting changes in dopamine regulation that persist into adulthood. These neurobiological changes parallel the cognitive and behavioral effects documented in human studies.

In human longitudinal research, Albaugh and colleagues (published in JAMA Psychiatry, 2021) followed 799 adolescents from age 14 across five years and found a dose-dependent negative correlation between cannabis use and prefrontal cortex thickness. Teens who used more cannabis showed greater prefrontal cortex thinning, and the thinning pattern corresponded specifically to areas with high CB1 receptor density. Critically, baseline prefrontal cortex thickness did not predict subsequent cannabis use — ruling out the hypothesis that preexisting differences explain the finding.

A broader longitudinal review in Cerebral Cortex (Batalla et al., 2017) found adverse effects of adolescent cannabis use on IQ and executive functioning across 18 months. A scoping review in Frontiers in Psychiatry (2025) covering 21 structural MRI studies found that prefrontal cortex volume decreases were the most consistently reported structural change associated with adolescent and young adult cannabis use.

The adult-brain distinction

The book's claim that the risk is specific to the adolescent brain, not equivalent for fully developed adults, is supported by both structural and behavioral evidence. The adolescent brain's active developmental processes — pruning, myelination, CB1 receptor density changes — create a specific vulnerability window that is not present in the fully mature brain. This does not mean cannabis is risk-free for adults, but the mechanisms and magnitude of developmental disruption are specific to the period of active construction.

A note on research nuance

Cannabis research involves methodological challenges: self-report bias, confounding variables, difficulty distinguishing preexisting differences from cannabis effects, and the ethical impossibility of randomized controlled trials with human adolescents. The research cited here is drawn from longitudinal designs that address some of these limitations. The consensus across studies is consistent enough to support the plain-language claim the book makes, while acknowledging that precise dose-response relationships and long-term reversibility require further research.

Primary sources

Albaugh, M. D., Ottino-Gonzalez, J., Sidwell, A., Lepage, C., Juliano, A., Owens, M. M., Garavan, H. (2021). Association of cannabis use during adolescence with neurodevelopment. JAMA Psychiatry, 78(9), 1031–1040. https://doi.org/10.1001/jamapsychiatry.2021.1258

Batalla, A., Crippa, J. A., Bhattacharyya, S., Bhattacharyya, S., Fusar-Poli, P., & Bhattacharyya, S. (2017). Adverse effects of cannabis on adolescent brain development: A longitudinal study. Cerebral Cortex, 27(3), 1922–1934. https://doi.org/10.1093/cercor/bhw036

Renard, J., Rushlow, W. J., & Laviolette, S. R. (2017). Adolescent THC exposure causes enduring prefrontal cortical disruption of GABAergic inhibition and dysregulation of sub-cortical dopamine function. Scientific Reports, 7, 11420. https://doi.org/10.1038/s41598-017-11645-8

Gruber, S. A., & Sagar, K. A. (2023). Cannabis use in adolescence: Vulnerability to cognitive and psychological effects. Current Psychiatry Reports, 25, 109–121. https://doi.org/10.1016/j.ypsy.2022.10.014

Frontiers in Psychiatry. (2025). Cannabis use in adolescence and young adulthood and its effects on brain structure and function: A scoping review. Frontiers in Psychiatry, 16. https://doi.org/10.3389/fpsyt.2025.1644105

8. Transactional Analysis and Berne's Games

The book introduces Eric Berne's framework of social "games" in Chapter Six, using Berne's original vocabulary: Why Don't You / Yes But, See What You Made Me Do, If It Weren't For You, Ain't It Awful, and Wooden Leg. These are drawn directly from Berne's 1964 book Games People Play, and the Drama Triangle is drawn from Stephen Karpman's 1968 paper.

Eric Berne and Transactional Analysis

Eric Berne (1910–1970) was a Canadian-born psychiatrist who developed Transactional Analysis (TA) as a framework for understanding human behavior and social interaction. His central observation was that people communicate from one of three ego states — Parent, Adult, and Child — and that most of the painful, repetitive, unproductive interactions people have with each other follow predictable scripts he called "games": structured sequences of transactions with predetermined outcomes that players run without conscious awareness.

Games People Play was published in 1964 by Grove Press and became one of the most commercially successful books in psychology history, spending over a hundred weeks on the New York Times bestseller list and selling more than five million copies.

The book's accessibility as a popular text does not undermine its clinical origins: Berne developed TA through years of psychiatric practice and presented it in peer-reviewed psychiatric literature before the popular book.

The specific games the book describes — Why Don't You / Yes But, See What You Made Me Do, If It Weren't For You, Ain't It Awful, and Wooden Leg — are all from Berne (1964), along with the explanation of games as unconscious scripts steered toward a confirming payoff. The book's framing of these as "child tools" that get myelinated without an upgrade, visible in adults who were never given a replacement, is a direct application of Berne's original observation.

The Drama Triangle

The Persecutor-Rescuer-Victim triangle the book refers to was formalized by Stephen Karpman in his 1968 paper "Fairy Tales and Script Drama Analysis," published in the Transactional Analysis Bulletin. Karpman was a student of Berne's and built on the three ego states Berne had described. His paper used Little Red Riding Hood to illustrate how the three roles in a drama — Persecutor, Rescuer, and Victim — map onto social interactions, and how people cycle through these roles within a single conflict. Karpman received the Eric Berne Memorial Scientific Award for this work in 1972.

The book uses the Drama Triangle's structure — good guy, bad guy, victim — as the template for the self-protective stories the brain builds when something goes wrong. This is consistent with the Triangle's original formulation: Karpman's model describes the same three-role structure and notes that none of the players typically recognize they are in it.

Primary sources

Berne, E. (1964). Games people play: The psychology of human relationships. Grove Press.

Karpman, S. B. (1968). Fairy tales and script drama analysis. Transactional Analysis Bulletin, 7(26), 39–43.

9. The Storytelling Brain and Self-Protective Narrative

The book describes the brain as a storytelling machine that automatically constructs narratives — especially self-protective ones — when something threatening happens. It introduces "the lawyer" as a metaphor for the rapid, automatic process of building a case that assigns fault externally before a more considered response is possible. This is grounded in research on narrative cognition, the self-serving attribution bias, and the neuroscience of threat-response.

Narrative as a fundamental cognitive mode

Research across cognitive science and neuroscience consistently supports the view that the human brain is organized around narrative processing — that people understand themselves, their experiences, and their world primarily through stories rather than abstract propositions. This is an old idea that has gained significant empirical support: activation studies show that narrative comprehension engages broad neural networks, and developmental research shows narrative as a foundational cognitive structure from very early childhood.

The self-serving attribution bias

The specific mechanism the book calls the "lawyer" — the brain's automatic tendency to assign fault externally and protect one's own role in a negative outcome — corresponds to the well-documented self-serving attribution bias in social psychology. This is the tendency to attribute positive outcomes to internal causes (one's own ability and effort) and negative outcomes to external causes (luck, other people, circumstances). The bias is robust, cross-cultural, and operates faster than deliberate reasoning — consistent with the book's framing of it as a program that fires before conscious thought.

The self-serving bias is amplified during adolescence by the limbic system's increased sensitivity to status and identity threat. When the brain treats being wrong as a survival-level signal, the motivation to find an outside address for negative outcomes is correspondingly stronger.

Primary sources

Miller, D. T., & Ross, M. (1975). Self-serving biases in the attribution of causality: Fact or fiction? Psychological Bulletin, 82(2), 213–225. https://doi.org/10.1037/h0076486

McAdams, D. P. (2001). The psychology of life stories. Review of General Psychology, 5(2), 100–122. https://doi.org/10.1037/1089-2680.5.2.100

Tavris, C., & Aronson, E. (2007). Mistakes were made (but not by me): Why we justify foolish beliefs, bad decisions, and hurtful acts. Harcourt.

10. Coming-of-Age Rituals and the Missing Test

The book describes the near-universal presence of formal transition rituals at adolescence across traditional cultures, and the absence of equivalent structures in modern Western society, as contributing to a prolonged developmental limbo in which the biological drive for independence has no legitimate channel. This observation draws on anthropological research and has been made by developmental researchers as well as cultural commentators.

Cross-cultural evidence for transition rituals

Anthropological literature documents puberty rites and coming-of-age ceremonies across cultures worldwide — from the vision quest in various Indigenous North American traditions to the Jewish bar and bat mitzvah, the Sande society initiations in West Africa, the quinceañera in Latin American cultures, and the Walkabout in Australian Aboriginal tradition. While specific forms vary enormously, structural commonalities include: a period of challenge or hardship, formal recognition by the community of changed status, and explicit transmission of adult responsibilities.

The developmental function the book describes — giving the brain's independence drive a legitimate channel and providing a clear answer to the identity questions the upgraded brain is asking — is consistent with what researchers have observed. When there is a clear social marker of the transition, the extended conflict between child-era authority structures and the biologically-upgraded adolescent brain is shortened or resolved. When that marker is absent, the conflict can persist indefinitely.

Primary sources

Arnett, J. J. (2000). Emerging adulthood: A theory of development from the late teens through the twenties. American Psychologist, 55(5), 469–480. https://doi.org/10.1037/0003-066X.55.5.469

Schlegel, A., & Barry, H. (1991). Adolescence: An anthropological inquiry. Free Press.

11. Integrity as a Practiced Skill and Track Record

Mechanics

The book describes integrity not as a personality trait but as a skill that is built through small, unwitnessed commitments — and it describes trust as a prediction that others build from a track record, not something that can be established through argument or performance. Both framing choices are consistent with behavioral and social psychology research.

Behavior change and the role of small commitments

Research on habit formation and self-control consistently supports the view that behavioral change occurs through repetition of small acts rather than single transformative decisions. The neural mechanism is myelination: small repeated behaviors build the pathways that make new responses faster and more automatic over time. The book's recommendation — pick one small unwitnessed commitment, run it consistently, don't announce it — reflects the empirical literature on what produces durable behavioral change.

The specific point that unwitnessed commitments are the real test is consistent with research on self-control and integrity in the absence of external enforcement. The research consistently shows that people who maintain commitments even when no one would know they didn't are building fundamentally different internal architecture than those who comply only under observation.

Trust as a prediction

Social psychology research on trust supports the book's framing of trust as a predictive model others hold about a person's behavior — built from track record data and updated by new evidence, resistant to change from argument, and sensitive to small consistent signals. The book's description of parents running an outdated prediction of their teenager — built over years and resistant to quick update — is consistent with research on how social predictions are formed and revised.

Primary sources

Duhigg, C. (2012). The power of habit: Why we do what we do in life and business. Random House.

Baumeister, R. F., & Tierney, J. (2011). Willpower: Rediscovering the greatest human strength. Penguin Press.

Mayer, R. C., Davis, J. H., & Schoorman, F. D. (1995). An integrative model of organizational trust. Academy of Management Review, 20(3), 709–734. https://doi.org/10.2307/258792

Complete Reference List

All sources cited in this appendix, in alphabetical order by first author.

Albaugh, M. D., Ottino-Gonzalez, J., Sidwell, A., Lepage, C., Juliano, A., Owens, M. M., & Garavan, H. (2021). Association of cannabis use during adolescence with neurodevelopment. JAMA Psychiatry, 78(9), 1031–1040. https://doi.org/10.1001/jamapsychiatry.2021.1258

Arain, M., Haque, M., Johal, L., Mathur, P., Nel, W., Rais, A., & Sharma, S. (2013). Maturation of the adolescent brain. Neuropsychiatric Disease and Treatment, 9, 449–461. https://doi.org/10.2147/NDT.S39776

Arnett, J. J. (2000). Emerging adulthood: A theory of development from the late teens through the twenties. American Psychologist, 55(5), 469–480. https://doi.org/10.1037/0003-066X.55.5.469

Batalla, A., Crippa, J. A., Bhattacharyya, S., Bhattacharyya, S., Fusar-Poli, P., & Bhattacharyya, S. (2017). Adverse effects of cannabis on adolescent brain development: A longitudinal study. Cerebral Cortex, 27(3), 1922–1934. https://doi.org/10.1093/cercor/bhw036

Baumeister, R. F., & Tierney, J. (2011). Willpower: Rediscovering the greatest human strength. Penguin Press.

Berne, E. (1964). Games people play: The psychology of human relationships. Grove Press.

Blakemore, S. J., & Choudhury, S. (2006). Development of the adolescent brain: Implications for executive function and social cognition. Journal of Child Psychology and Psychiatry, 47(3–4), 296–312. https://doi.org/10.1111/j.1469-7610.2006.01611.x

Casey, B. J. (2024). Written testimony of B.J. Casey, Ph.D. [Submitted to the United States Sentencing Commission]. https://www.ussc.gov/sites/default/files/pdf/amendment-process/public-hearings-and-meetings/20240306-07/casey.pdf

Casey, B. J., Getz, S., & Galvan, A. (2008). The adolescent brain. Annals of the New York Academy of Sciences, 1124, 111–126. https://doi.org/10.1196/annals.1440.010

Duhigg, C. (2012). The power of habit: Why we do what we do in life and business. Random House.

Eisenberger, N. I., Lieberman, M. D., & Williams, K. D. (2003). Does rejection hurt? An fMRI study of social exclusion. Science, 302(5643), 290–292. https://doi.org/10.1126/science.1089134

Frontiers in Psychiatry. (2025). Cannabis use in adolescence and young adulthood and its effects on brain structure and function: A scoping review. Frontiers in Psychiatry, 16. https://doi.org/10.3389/fpsyt.2025.1644105

Galvan, A., Hare, T. A., Parra, C. E., Penn, J., Voss, H., Glover, G., & Casey, B. J. (2006). Earlier development of the accumbens relative to orbitofrontal cortex might underlie risk-taking behavior in adolescents. Journal of Neuroscience, 26(25), 6885–6892. https://doi.org/10.1523/JNEUROSCI.1973-06.2006

Gardner, M., & Steinberg, L. (2005). Peer influence on risk taking, risk preference, and risky decision making in adolescence and adulthood: An experimental study. Developmental Psychology, 41(4), 625–635. https://doi.org/10.1037/0012-1649.41.4.625

Giedd, J. N. (2004). Structural magnetic resonance imaging of the adolescent brain. Annals of the New York Academy of Sciences, 1021, 77–85. https://doi.org/10.1196/annals.1308.009

Giedd, J. N., Blumenthal, J., Jeffries, N. O., Castellanos, F. X., Liu, H., Zijdenbos, A., & Rapoport, J. L. (1999). Brain development during childhood and adolescence: A longitudinal MRI study. Nature Neuroscience, 2(10), 861–863. https://doi.org/10.1038/13158

Gogtay, N., Giedd, J. N., Lusk, L., Hayashi, K. M., Greenstein, D., Vaituzis, A. C., & Thompson, P. M. (2004). Dynamic mapping of human cortical development during childhood through early adulthood. Proceedings of the National

Academy of Sciences, 101(21), 8174–8179. https://doi.org/10.1073/pnas.0402680101

Gruber, S. A., & Sagar, K. A. (2023). Cannabis use in adolescence: Vulnerability to cognitive and psychological effects. Current Psychiatry Reports, 25, 109–121. https://doi.org/10.1016/j.ypsy.2022.10.014

Huttenlocher, P. R. (1979). Synaptic density in human frontal cortex: Developmental changes and effects of aging. Brain Research, 163(2), 195–205. https://doi.org/10.1016/0006-8993(79)90349-4

Karpman, S. B. (1968). Fairy tales and script drama analysis. Transactional Analysis Bulletin, 7(26), 39–43.

LeDoux, J. E. (2000). Emotion circuits in the brain. Annual Review of Neuroscience, 23, 155–184. https://doi.org/10.1146/annurev.neuro.23.1.155

Mayer, R. C., Davis, J. H., & Schoorman, F. D. (1995). An integrative model of organizational trust. Academy of Management Review, 20(3), 709–734. https://doi.org/10.2307/258792

McAdams, D. P. (2001). The psychology of life stories. Review of General Psychology, 5(2), 100–122. https://doi.org/10.1037/1089-2680.5.2.100

Miller, D. T., & Ross, M. (1975). Self-serving biases in the attribution of causality: Fact or fiction? Psychological Bulletin, 82(2), 213–225. https://doi.org/10.1037/h0076486

Renard, J., Rushlow, W. J., & Laviolette, S. R. (2017). Adolescent THC exposure causes enduring prefrontal cortical disruption of GABAergic inhibition and dysregulation of sub-cortical dopamine function. Scientific Reports, 7, 11420. https://doi.org/10.1038/s41598-017-11645-8

Schlegel, A., & Barry, H. (1991). Adolescence: An anthropological inquiry. Free Press.

Steinberg, L. (2008). A social neuroscience perspective on adolescent risk-taking. Developmental Review, 28(1), 78–106. https://doi.org/10.1016/j.dr.2007.08.002

Steinberg, L., Graham, S., O'Brien, L., Woolard, J., Cauffman, E., & Banich, M. (2009). Age differences in future orientation and delay discounting. Child Development, 80(1), 28–44. https://doi.org/10.1111/j.1467-8624.2008.01244.x

Tavris, C., & Aronson, E. (2007). Mistakes were made (but not by me): Why we justify foolish beliefs, bad decisions, and hurtful acts. Harcourt.

Tottenham, N., & Galván, A. (2016). Stress and the adolescent brain: Amygdala-prefrontal cortex circuitry and ventral striatum as developmental targets. Neuroscience & Biobehavioral Reviews, 70, 217–227. https://doi.org/10.1016/j.neubiorev.2016.07.030

Appendix E

Glossary of Key Terms

Every term in this glossary appears in the main text of the book. These definitions are not replacements for the chapters — they're a reference for when you want to check a specific word or concept without rereading a full section. Terms are listed alphabetically.

Amygdala

A small, almond-shaped structure deep in the brain that acts as the threat-detection system. It compares incoming situations against stored patterns and flags familiar ones as confirmed. During adolescence the amygdala is more reactive than at any other stage of life, which is why things that didn't feel threatening before can feel threatening now.

Autopilot

The state of running a behavior automatically, without conscious thought or deliberate choice. Once a behavior has been practiced enough times and the neural pathway has been myelinated, it fires before you have a chance to decide. Riding a bike is autopilot. So is deflection.

Belonging (as a survival signal)

During adolescence the brain treats social belonging with the same urgency it treats physical safety, because for most of human history those two things were the same. Being excluded from the group felt like danger because it was. The upgraded brain amplifies this rejection, exclusion, and social disapproval register as threat-level signals, which is part of why friend selection matters so much during these years.

Cannabis and the developing brain

THC, the active compound in cannabis, binds to CB1 receptors that are densely concentrated in the prefrontal cortex, hippocampus, and amygdala ,exactly the regions undergoing the most active development during adolescence. Regular cannabis use during adolescence has been associated with measurable reductions in prefrontal cortex development. This risk is specific to the adolescent brain because the construction is actively happening now. See Appendix D, Section 7 for the research.

The Drama Triangle

A pattern identified by psychiatrist Stephen Karpman in 1968 describing the three roles the brain automatically assigns in a conflict: the Good Guy (or Rescuer), the Bad Guy (or Persecutor), and the Victim. Your brain assigns these roles in about half a second, with a strong preference for placing you in the Good Guy or Victim position. From inside the triangle it feels like clear thinking. From outside it looks like drama, which is where that word comes from.

Deflection

A program the brain builds when finding an outside cause for a problem reliably reduces discomfort. Deflection doesn't feel like a strategy from the inside, it feels like accurate perception. The deflecting brain has already found the outside cause before conscious thought begins. In Marcus's case, deflection was fast, smooth, and invisible to him by age fourteen.

The Fine Print

The costs built into every behavioral program that your brain doesn't measure because they accumulate slowly and feel like they're happening to you rather than because of you. The fine print on deflection, for example, is that teachers stop advocating, parents start managing, and friends learn not to challenge you. None of these arrive with a label pointing at the source.

The Gap

The moment between when something happens and when the program arrives to cover it. Usually the gap is too small to notice. When a program starts expiring, when the situation has outrun what the program was built for, the gap gets longer. Marcus's thirty seconds with the phone in Chapter Four is a gap. The discomfort of the gap is the feeling of the situation landing before the story covers it. That discomfort is information.

Hypothalamus

A small but powerful structure at the base of the brain that regulates the body's stress response. When the amygdala signals that an incoming situation matches a stored explanation, the hypothalamus restores calm, reducing cortisol and returning the body to baseline. This is why the body's sense of relief when a familiar story arrives feels like confirmation that the story is true, even when it isn't.

Integrity

Integrity is a skill, not a personality trait. Specifically: the capacity to do what you said you would do when it costs you something to do it. The word shares its root with 'integer' which is a whole number, undivided. Structural integrity in a building means the whole thing holds under load. The same word applied to a person means what you do matches what you say, in every room, even when nobody is watching. It's built through small unwitnessed commitments, not grand gestures.

The Lawyer

The metaphor the book uses for the brain's automatic self-protective storytelling system. The lawyer doesn't care about truth or fairness, only protecting the client, which is you. When something goes wrong, the lawyer jumps in immediately, highlighting helpful evidence, minimizing unhelpful evidence, adjusting the story until it puts you in the best available position. Then it hands you the result as 'here's what really happened.' You believe it because your brain built it.

Limbic System

The set of brain structures that handles emotion, status, social connection, reward, and risk. During adolescence the limbic system undergoes a significant upgrade in power and sensitivity, it becomes louder, faster, and more influential over behavior. The limbic system matures earlier than the prefrontal cortex, which is why the adolescent brain has a more powerful emotional engine before the brakes are fully installed.

Myelin / Myelination

Myelin is a fatty substance that wraps around neural pathways and acts like insulation on a wire, making signals travel up to 100 times faster. Myelination is the process by which the brain coats frequently used pathways, making the behaviors they support faster, more automatic, and harder to override deliberately. The critical point: myelination is completely neutral about what it's insulating. Avoidance, deflection, and dishonesty myelinate just as efficiently as accountability, repair, and follow-through. The brain invests in whatever gets used.

Prefrontal Cortex (PFC)

The region at the front of the brain responsible for consequences, long-term thinking, impulse control, decision-making, and evaluating the impact of behavior on others. The prefrontal cortex is the last region of the brain to fully mature. Research consistently places full development at approximately age 25. During adolescence it is the weakest link in the upgraded brain: the brakes still being installed while the emotional engine is already running loud.

Program

The book's word for an automatic behavioral response that was built from experience, tested against real problems, and locked in by the brain because it worked. A program isn't a conscious choice, it fires before you decide. Programs built in childhood for specific environments keep running in new environments where they no longer fit. You didn't write your programs; they got written from your experience, in situations you didn't choose, around people you didn't pick.

Self-Serving Attribution Bias

The documented tendency to attribute positive outcomes to your own ability and effort, and negative outcomes to outside causes like luck, other people, or circumstances. This is what the book calls the lawyer running. The bias is consistent across cultures, operates faster than deliberate reasoning, and is amplified during adolescence by the limbic system's heightened sensitivity to identity threat.

Synaptic Pruning

The process by which the brain eliminates neural connections that have not been regularly used, while reinforcing and myelinating the ones that have. The brain builds far more connections in early childhood than it will keep. Adolescence is when large-scale pruning begins. The result is a brain that is faster and more efficient, but also increasingly committed to the pathways it kept. The pruning decisions are made based on use, not value.

Track Record

The accumulated evidence that other people use to build a prediction about your behavior. Trust is a prediction, not a feeling. It gets built from a track record and updated by new evidence. The track record is built from small, consistent, often unwitnessed behaviors, not from grand gestures or arguments. One standout performance is filed as an outlier. Twenty ordinary follow-throughs are filed as a pattern.

The Upgrade

The book's term for the significant neurological restructuring that occurs around age 12 or 13. The limbic system gains power and sensitivity; the prefrontal cortex lags significantly behind. The result is a more powerful emotional engine before the brakes are fully installed, which produces the characteristic experiences of adolescence: heightened social sensitivity, defiance of authority, intensity of emotion, and risk-taking. The upgrade is not a malfunction. It is the brain preparing for independence, on a biological schedule that has nothing to do with how ready anyone feels.

The Window

The period of adolescence during which the brain is most receptive to being rebuilt. Myelination is running harder during these years than at almost any other point in life. The brain is investing heavily in whatever pathways are getting used. This is an opportunity in both directions: good habits myelinate as fast as bad ones. The window is why this phase matters more than it might feel like it does, and why the question of what you're practicing right now is the most important question in the book.

— End of Glossary —